FROM THE WALL TO THE WATER

A JOURNEY THROUGH ASIA

WILLIAM HAN

EARNSHAW
BOOKS

From the Wall to the Water

William Han

ISBN-13: 978-988-8769-51-3

TRAVEL / Asia / General

EB166

Published by Earnshaw Books Ltd. (Hong Kong)

1

THE JOURNEY OF TEN THOUSAND MILES

HALFWAY ACROSS the bridge to Afghanistan, I paused and looked back upon whence I'd come.

The bridge was deserted. The Uzbek soldiers who had interrogated me just a few minutes earlier were now too far back to see. Their Afghan counterparts were equally too far in front of me. It was a cloudless day at this spot near the midpoint of the Eurasian landmass. The August sun shone hot on my face. Sweat gathered where the frame of my sunglasses met my temples. The river beneath my feet, the Amu Darya, rolled on impenetrably muddy. It seemed to conceal a millennium's worth of pain.

I took out my phone and snapped a surreptitious photo of the bridge, evidence for myself that I had indeed come here and stood on this structure. Surreptitious because soldiers were often skittish about people photographing the borders they guarded. Did any spy still take photos of borders instead of using Google Earth? Moments ago, the Uzbeks had treated me like a spy. I looked around for snipers and found none, but still.

I wanted to memorialize this passage, not only because of what I knew lay ahead but because of the history that took place here. The Soviet Army retreated across this bridge at the end of their Afghan adventure. I pictured the Russian general standing just about where I stood. Perhaps he paused and looked back on the bloodied and scarred country he was leaving behind, the same way I was now looking forward to it.

Putting the phone back in my pocket, I felt the weight of my backpack more than usually and paused to adjust its straps. Unnecessarily, of course, but the act delayed the inevitable. Because I was afraid.

There was every possibility that I was making a horrible mistake. The country at the end of this bridge was a war zone. If a car bomb were to go off and I happened to be passing by, that would be it. If I were to get caught in the middle of a firefight, that would probably be it. If the Taliban decided to kidnap me, then I would have to get used to wearing an orange jumpsuit.

I was far from home in this unlikely spot in the summer of 2015. But then again, I had lived my entire life in some sense or other far from home. The permanent migrant, the perpetual wanderer.

But I couldn't tarry in no man's land forever. Onward.

At the other end of the bridge, a handsome Afghan officer in military uniform stood at his post. He spoke without looking up: "Passport."

I took out my New Zealand passport with the distinctive silver fern on its black cover and slid it across. He saw it with surprise and only then looked up to see my foreign features.

He stretched out one hand and bellowed with good cheer: "Welcome to Afghanistan."

*****

I had reached a crossroads in my life. I was born in Taiwan, today still officially called the "Republic of China," as opposed to the "People's Republic," which is what people mean when they say "China." My grandparents were veterans of World War II and the Chinese Civil War that followed, on the anti-communist, losing side. Having lost, they escaped to Taiwan like Aeneas out of burning Troy. There they brought up their children in the modest circumstances of defeated soldiers.

When I was twelve, my parents decided to pack up and move to New Zealand. I didn't speak much English then. The school stuck me in remedial class with the kids who couldn't tell time looking at a clock or had yet to grasp multiplication. I spent a lot of time pretending I understood what people said to me before deducing their meaning from context. Six years later, I graduated from high school at the top of my class. I applied for colleges in the U.S. and went to Yale and later Columbia Law School. Then I stayed in New York City to practice law.

By 2015, however, it grew increasingly apparent that the byzantine U.S. immigration system would not allow me to stay in the country. The prospect of having to leave behind the life that I'd built prompted a period of reflection, even depression. And I had turned thirty-three by then. The same age, as I pointed out too frequently, that Jesus was when he died. More or less the same age as Dante when he wrote these lines: "Midway upon the journey of our life / I found myself within a forest dark, / For the straightforward pathway had been lost."

I was working at a genteel law firm that paid me more money than was reasonable. I had enough savings, in fact, that if I lived frugally and chose a modestly priced location (so not Manhattan), I might not need to ever work again—as long as I remained a party of one.

By this time, I had been seeing Ashley on and off for over two years. The sort of woman who caused other men to glare at me resentfully, she was a Southern belle, the WASP daughter of a Navy captain from Virginia. We had met during happy hour at a bar on the ground floor of the Empire State Building, where she asked a friend of hers to introduce us.

One night during the course of our relationship, she and I went to a party together, where she drank a bit more than she should have. I took her home to her apartment building on Riverside Drive.

I cannot recall how this particular conversation started, but the salient part went like this:

Ashley: "I'm white; you're Asian. That means you're reaching and I'm settling. You will never break up with me, because I'm the best you can ever do."

Me: "In that case, we should break up."

Ashley: "No wait—"

In the end I decided to wait at least for sobriety and the light of day. In the morning, I reported her own words back to her. She promised that she had no recollection of them and begged for forgiveness. To my shame, I agreed. How many relationships continue in this way, out of one or both parties' fear of being alone?

But not for a moment could I forget that, as the Romans used to say, "In vino veritas." Uncle Sam would allow me to stay if Ashley and I got married. But, because I could never forget what she said, I could never think that marriage to her would be a good idea.

I would remain a party of one.

At times, Ashley seemed to try to make up for what she said. One year for Chinese New Year she gave me a red envelope that she picked up in Chinatown—just the empty envelope, with nothing in it: She didn't realize that the point of the custom was to put something inside. She also often told me that she wanted to see China, hopefully with me by her side showing her around.

Nevertheless, on that inebriated night, she had touched on a question that had haunted me for most of my life. Who, or what, is an Asian man in a white man's world? Particular one

4

like me, neither fresh off the boat nor an actual Asian-American? What was my place in it? Did I have one at all? The confluence of circumstances urged me to set out into the wider world to seek the answer.

A decade earlier, shortly after college, I had discovered the value of travel where many other young people have done for years, in Southeast Asia. The lush jungles of Thailand, the slow boat drifting down the Mekong through Laos, and the splendors of Angkor Wat in Cambodia were among my formative experiences as an adult traveler. That and subsequent trips taught me the wisdom of Ishmael's statement in *Moby Dick* — whenever it is a damp, drizzly November in my soul, then, I account it high time to get to sea as soon as I can. My soul had rarely felt damper than in the spring of 2015.

"The journey of ten thousand miles begins with a single step" — so goes the Chinese proverb that Westerners like to quote so much. Another Chinese proverb goes like this: "The journey of ten thousand miles is better than the study of ten thousand volumes." I decided to find out whether that was true and take the first step.

And, in considering this first step, I remembered a man named Gan Ying whom I had read about even as a child.

In the late first century, Han Dynasty (202 B.C — 220 A.D.) China fought a decisive campaign against the fierce Xiongnu, whom some historians have identified with the infamous Huns who would later ravage Europe. In the wake of Han victory, they began migrating away from the Chinese frontier. Suddenly, the westward way to Europe was open. And General Ban Chao, who led the Chinese army against them, had an idea: Someone ought to go and see what lay at the other end of the Silk Road, that ancient artery running the length of the Eurasian landmass.

Ban Chao remains a legend even today. In one battle, deep

behind enemy lines, he won a brilliant victory with only thirty-six of his best soldiers, the ancient Chinese equivalent of the Navy SEALs. On that occasion, the great general added a new proverb to the Chinese language: "One who fears to enter the tiger's den cannot return with a tiger cub."

Freshly famous and victorious, Ban Chao could authorize even the most unlikely undertakings. He reviewed his thirty-six brave companions and picked out the right man for the epic expedition in search of the Roman Empire: Gan Ying.

The year was 97 A.D. No Chinese had ever reached Roman territory before. The country of Caesar to him was no more than a tall tale told by tarrying travelers, a whispered rumor spread next to campfires on the grassy steppes. Nonetheless he went, a quest for a phantom land that might or might not be.

I identified with Gan Ying. He was an Eastern man who tried to reach the heart of the Western world, Rome, and he got turned around in the final stretch. I am a sort of Eastern man who reached the heart of the modern Western world, New York City, and I got turned around in the final stretch before being allowed to stay long term.

And his journey joined the Orient and the Occident. Through the lens of him, it seemed to me, there was no Eastern history or Western history; there was a single universal history from which we all sprang. The idea appealed to me as a creature of both East and West.

I began to spend my evenings researching the route he might have taken, with the idea of retracing it. Gan Ying traveled farther than any of his countrymen had ever done, "beyond what was recorded in the *Shan Hai Jing*" — "The Book of Mountains and Seas." That anonymously authored tract of real and mythological biology and geography was compiled over as many as twenty centuries and represented the sum total of Chinese knowledge at the time of the world beyond the borders of their country.

Another text, the *Hou Han Shu*, or "History of the Later Han Dynasty," recorded Gan Ying's journey and served as my lodestar. Written in the 5th century by the historian Fan Hua, it distilled the imperial annals from the first and second centuries into a coherent narrative. Among its sources was the report that Gan Ying made to the emperor upon his return.

I matched the place names mentioned in the *Hou Han Shu* with their often harsher modern equivalents. The old names, redolent with mystery, began to take on an incantatory quality as I noted them down one by one: Tashkurgan (still called Tashkurgan, now on the China-Pakistan Highway), Alexandria Prophthasia (now Farah, Afghanistan), Arsacid (that ancient dynasty of Persia), Hecatompylos (in eastern Iran), Antiochia in Persis (now the city of Bushehr on the Persian Gulf)—saying these words out loud, on the tongue they felt like spells out of a dusty grimoire.

And Rome itself, referred to as "Daqin" or "Great Qin" in the *Hou Han Shu*. "Qin" was the name of China's first imperial dynasty and the ultimate source of the English word "China." In other words, the Chinese called the Roman Empire "Great China." The Middle Kingdom never paid another country a more sincere compliment than that.

But—ah, what is that country along the path? Afghanistan was a war zone. Bullets flew and bombs blew.

And what did I have going for me? I was a bookish, overeducated guy who could barely run half a mile without getting winded. Growing up and pre-laser eye surgery, I had terrible eyesight and wore glasses, which discouraged me from playing sports. The sight of fifteen-year-old me stumbling after a soccer ball would've brought tears to your eyes. I used to joke (was it a joke?) that chess was my sport. I never did military service anywhere and didn't know how to use a gun. Racial stereotyping aside, I had taken all of one semester's worth of judo, back in college.

By ordinary standards, I was a fairly experienced traveler, having spent time in thirty-odd countries by then. But I'd never ventured into an active war zone, never climbed K2, never swum the English Channel. I was no Livingstone or Shackleton.

In Afghanistan, I would have nothing more than my wits to protect me, only such knowledge of local culture as I could gain as a quick study, only the judgment to know the difference between the intrepid and the stupid. That and a big smile and a firm handshake.

But if ever I had come to a crisis point in my life, this was it. If ever I felt an inexorable force pushing me outward into the world and onto some quest, this was that moment. The mission to travel from the yellow earth of China to the green pastures of Kyrgyzstan, from the ancient cities of Uzbekistan through the ruins of Afghanistan, and from the grandeur of Iran to the splendors of Italy, now seemed inescapable. Nothing else, for the moment, mattered.

2

A STUDY IN OCHRE

"You have a book in there."

Said the border official, pointing at my backpack that had just gone through the dusty X-ray machine. She was in her thirties, medium height and build. In and of herself she would not have been particularly intimidating, perhaps a somewhat unpleasant civics teacher at a local middle school. In her uniform, however, she represented the arm of the Chinese state and its awesome power.

"Do I?" I answered. Then I immediately surmised that she was not one to appreciate witty repartee.

"I need to know what it is," she snarled, baring her jaundiced teeth.

What dangerous material could I possibly have brought? The Tiananmen Papers? For a brief moment I wondered if I had thoughtlessly carried something with me that could attract Beijing's ire. For all my previous travels in China, it had not occurred to me this time around to review the reading materials in my backpack for political sensitivity.

I opened my bag and produced a collection of Paul Theroux's travel writings that my friend Marina gave me as a parting gift.

"Dangerous stuff," I mumbled.

"Not that one," the dour officer shook her head. "There's

another book in there, bigger. Show me."

I dug deeper into my backpack and produced my copy of *Lonely Planet China*. I put it in front of the officer. "It's a guidebook," I stated the obvious.

She waved me past with what sounded to me almost like a snort. I could just about see the contemptuous thought bubble coming out of her skull: What kind of fake-foreigner-Chinese carries an English-language guidebook to come to China?

Ah, yes, I had returned. The most dangerous contraband I could bring into this country was not weapons or drugs but a banned book. They weren't wrong. Ideas are the most dangerous things in the world. At this time, neither Google nor Gmail nor YouTube nor Facebook nor Twitter nor the New York Times nor the Wall Street Journal was accessible on the Chinese Internet.

This encounter should have been my first clue, the first entry in the case file. But I didn't realize yet that, like a Holmes or a Marlowe, I was about to be faced with a case to solve.

*****

But this was merely the China of today and the China of reality. It was neither the China of the past nor that of our dreams. The latter often reminded me of those famous lines by Tennyson:

> *We are not now that strength which in old days*
> *Moved earth and heaven, that which we are, we are;*
> *One equal temper of heroic hearts,*
> *Made weak by time and fate, but strong in will*
> *To strive, to seek, to find, and not to yield.*

My father always described us as Chinese, even though he had barely been born at the time my grandparents took him to Taiwan at the end of the Chinese Civil War in 1949. It often seemed like he only wanted to talk about the events surrounding that moment of exile. The man had lived his entire life in the shadow of traumatic occurrences that by rights he should not have been able to remember.

The China to which my father felt he belonged, however, did not exist, had not existed for many years, and maybe never existed in the first place. Certainly by now it existed solely as an ephemera in a dreamscape shared by some descendants of those soldiers of the lost Republic. The one that had a bill of rights in its constitution. The one that was the second country in the world to grant women the right to vote. The one that fought alongside the Allies in both world wars.

But as a dreamscape it is not to be dismissed so lightly. The Chinese are a people defined by their history to an extent unique among human societies. They remember their past, the words and deeds of ancient emperors and generals and poets and philosophers whose bones have long turned to dust. Sure, the reality today might be a far cry from the historical memory of those past ages of glory, which is surely idealized. But nonetheless there is an ideal. They are a people who remember that there is greatness in them, even if only an imagined greatness from an imagined past in a retroactively imagined community.

Gan Ying made his madcap quest for Rome during the Han Dynasty. Even today the Chinese still speak of "the divine majesty of the Han, the great prosperity of the Tang," referring to the two eras of which they are most proud. Indeed, the dynasty is the reason that the demonym for the majority race in China is "Han." (Though the word shouldn't be confused with my surname, which is a homonym.) They remember, or imagine that they remember, the old days when they, like Rome at its height, really seemed capable of moving earth and heaven. And they see plainly what time and fate have wrought.

Perhaps today China is resurgent, ready to be that strength once more. But if there is one thing that the Chinese understand, it is that this too shall pass. All good things come to an end, and all dark nights must give way to the dawn. The glories of the Han and the Tang came and went, as did the "century of humiliation" that began with the First Opium War.

Families like mine hope against hope that the cause of their grandparents might not be irretrievable after all. Perhaps they had planted such seeds of ideas that won't fully flourish for another century, or two, or three. Victory three hundred years hence is victory nonetheless. Three hundred years is no more than the average length of a dynasty, and we've watched a dozen of those come and go. Our job in any individual, puny lifetime is no more and no less than to strive, to seek, to find, and not to yield.

On the other hand, this country is too old, these people are too jaded and too shaped by their history, not to realize that the good and the right and the just do not always, or even often, prevail. There has never been a shortage of injustice in China. Indeed, the greatest crimes have always been the ones most likely to escape punishment.

To follow Gan Ying, I would need to head to Xinjiang, the vast northwestern section of the country, where the Chinese portion of the Silk Road properly began. But a couple of preliminary stops first, and with Ashley beside me: Once I told her of my travel plans, she asked to accompany me for the China portion of the journey. Given how much she had spoken of wanting to visit this country, I agreed.

To begin with, we would visit my family's ancestral home. Family lore, as I had heard and understood it, stated that in the third year of the reign of the Ming founder the Hongwu Emperor, or 1371, a certain General Han relocated from his home farther north when he was posted to a section of the province of Hubei on the north bank of the Yangtze River. On my father's side, we are all his descendants.

The area, formerly known as the "Han Family's Peninsula," now "Han Bay," was about an hour's drive outside of the central-Chinese metropolis of Wuhan. Four and half years after this visit, the novel coronavirus was first identified here.

Just one more thing that I could not foresee.

*****

I feel honor-bound here to take a paragraph or two to speak in defense of the land of my ancestors. In the minds of Westerners who had never heard of Wuhan until they also heard of the coronavirus, the city became a metonym for disease. But that's the equivalent of saying that, to people who never heard of Chicago until they also heard of the mob, Chicago is synonymous with crime.

Of course, the Chinese themselves know Wuhan as readily as Americans know Chicago. And the cities are roughly comparable in importance and function, each the economic center of a large swath of the middle of the country. Except Wuhan is by far the senior, just as China is much older than America. The oldest excavated township in the area dates back some 3,500 years.

During the long centuries of the Spring and Autumn (771 – 476 B.C.) and Warring States (476 – 221 B.C.) periods, when China was not one country but a series of medium-sized kingdoms, Hubei fell within the Kingdom of Chu. It was the southernmost of the five – then seven – major warring kingdoms that divided China. The Chu laid much of the foundation of what we now know of as Chinese civilization. *The Songs of Chu*, an anthology of poetry from this kingdom, became a foundational text of Chinese literature that influenced all that was to come. If you enjoy dragon boat racing, then you owe it to the people of Chu, who invented the sport as far back as 500 B.C.

Though eventually defeated and conquered by the Kingdom of Qin, which became China's first imperial dynasty, the people of Chu had their revenge just a couple of decades later: They led the revolution that overthrew the Qin to establish the Han Dynasty, the one that we're all so proud of. Both the imperial family of the Han as well as the chief architects of that regime— hence the architects of imperial government as a concept for the next two millennia—were from this area.

Fast forward to 1911, and the spirit of rebellion still prevailed here. For years during the tail end of the nineteenth and the beginning of the twentieth centuries, democratic revolutionaries had plotted uprisings against the corrupt, failing Qing Empire of the Manchus. But the imperial regime violently suppressed their every attempt, executing many idealistic young people in the process. It was in Wuhan in October 1911 that the luck of the revolutionaries finally turned. And once this city dared to fire the first shots, the rest of the country quickly followed and raised the banner of freedom. Just like that, over two thousand years of monarchy came to an end, and the Republic was born.

I beg you, then: the next time you think of Wuhan, think of it as the city of history and culture, of literature and liberty, not just as the launching pad of a pandemic.

*****

Seen from the air, the Hubei countryside gave the overwhelming impression of dirt. The Chinese call their country the "yellow earth," and they mean it quite literally. Mounds of dirt were strewn about the airport, like open sores or festering wounds, doing nothing and having nothing done to them in particular. On the drive into the city, dusty winds encrusted my face with a layer of yellow grime. Government trucks sprayed water on the roads in a quixotic attempt to bring the dust under control. It was as though the yellow earth itself meant to cling to these people, to drag them down to the mud, like some half-mad and smothering mother keeping her kids in arrested development, lest they should dare to fly toward some adulthood of higher aspirations.

I took surreptitious glances at Ashley in the car beside me. She looked tense in the face of such unfamiliar surroundings as we sped through the ocherous Hubei countryside.

I had never been to Han Bay before, and I had never met any of the people there, but I'd been told that half the population in this town were related to me somehow. After all, it was named after us. The idea that I might visit here pleased my father a great deal. Even though he also never came here until the late 1980s, when he was around forty, he always referred to the town as "old home," as though he'd grown up here with deep and fond memories of swimming in the river and playing in the fields. He contacted a cousin and asked him to meet us.

My cousin the cab driver met us at our hotel in Wuhan. "Hello, hello, welcome," Pingsheng said with profuse friendliness upon greeting us, if also a measure of apprehension. The blonde next to me was a deeply alien presence to him, as I nearly was as well. To help to put him at ease, as we drove out of the city, I asked innocuous questions about how things had developed in the area in recent years.

His name meant "peaceful life," or more negatively, "uneventful life." Though more than a decade and half older than I, he was of my generation on the family tree, being the grandson of my grandfather's older brother. Locating one's place in the genealogy was everything, so much so that most of the relatives I would meet on this day never told me their names — all that mattered was that we addressed each other with the correct forms of address that denoted our relative positions on the sprawling branches. And by "correct" I mean slightly incorrect — it was also customary to address each other one degree more familiarly than was technically accurate. Pingsheng addressed me as a brother.

To say that he was forty-nine is to say that he was born in 1966, the first year of the Cultural Revolution. And he showed the marks of that harder life that he'd led and that I would never know. His hair had thinned without leaving a precise bald spot. One front tooth was broken, so that when he smiled a jagged aperture opened at the center of his mouth. When he spoke of my branch of the family, which is to say my grandfather's descendants, he spoke with wistfulness, imagining the gentler lives that we must have led. Having grown up in an age of chaos, perhaps the best that anyone could reasonably hope for was an uneventful life.

He became a taxi driver years ago when my father helped him buy his first cab. In the early years of economic reform, these kinsmen of ours lived in abject poverty, and my father took pleasure in helping them and maybe also in lording it over them. The favor he owed my father was why he now played my host.

But on this day, Pingsheng was driving his private car. And he had his fifteen-year-old daughter in tow, a petite, vivacious girl with braces who called me uncle. The Chinese were bourgeois now with their two cars and their orthodontics. She asked if Ashley and I might choose an English name for her, and we decided on Hillary, after Rodham Clinton. She enjoyed the association. Together we set out for Yingcheng, the town of 700,000 (a hamlet by Chinese standards) of which Han Bay was a suburb.

On the way, Pingsheng informed me that my great-grandfather had been a lawyer like me, a litigator who was famous throughout the province. I was dubious about this claim, both because I had never heard it before, and because as far as I understood, there were no "lawyers" in imperial China. There were relatively educated men who assisted other men with court proceedings, like prototypical lawyers in medieval Europe, but they were never lawyers in the modern sense of the word.

As far as I knew, my great-grandfather was instead a clever student (attaining the "juren" or provincial degree of the civil service exam) and shrewd businessman who forsook the farm work passed down to him to begin a mining empire. Of course, the money didn't last—when the Communists took over, they confiscated all the mines.

But the idea fascinated me, nonetheless, that I had inherited something from my great-grandfather, something that couldn't be confiscated, without knowing it.

Later, shown the two-volume family tree in the middle of a farmhouse, I found this legend next to my great-grandfather's name: "... born January 6, 1868, date of death unclear. From a young age he studied Confucian scholarship, understood people's hearts, so that when faced with difficult disputes he was able to resolve them with only one or two words." Turned out my great-grandfather was indeed some kind of a lawyer, besides being a mine operator.

But I get ahead of myself.

We made a stop at Pingsheng's home. It was a spacious enough apartment on the fourth floor of a new-ish concrete building. Poetry about tea decorated the walls of the living room. A flat-screen TV faced the couch. But for the decrepit elevator, smelling faintly of long-ago urine with two sides of which being two-by-fours nailed into planks, and the impoverished-looking lobby, one would have said that he and his family lived in very comfortable surroundings. Unthinkable luxury a generation earlier.

Hillary and I played a game of Chinese chess on the coffee table, which I handily won only to feel apologetic for not even faking a little. Pingsheng's wife brought out plate after plate of fresh fruit. She and Ashley blushed at each other, one discomfited by the rare foreign guest and the other surprised to find herself in a small corner of China. She wasn't in Virginia anymore.

Pingsheng noted that it would befit my traditional filial duty to pay my respects at my grandfather's tomb. At a funeral shop run by the father-in-law of another cousin, this one a bus driver, we picked up bundles of paper money for the dead, incense sticks, and firecrackers.

Finally we went to the farmhouse in Han Bay where my grandfather had grown up, where he was eventually interred after he passed away in Taiwan. The stones of its walls presumably once formed an orderly lattice, but no more; now they looked like Lego blocks belonging to a young child who had not the patience to put them together properly. And its clay-tiled roofline sagged badly, bordering on collapse.

I had seen this type of surroundings before in my travels, but it always jarred me, and certainly it jarred me no less now that I knew the people living in it and knew them to be related to me by blood.

It and other old farmhouses huddled on the land side of the "peninsula," which was really the tract of land surrounded on three sides by a bend in the river. Toward the river, farmers wielded scythes over their crops, their chests bare, conical bamboo hats over their heads, as dozens of generations of their ancestors had done before them.

Trash was strewn about the house and on the floor in the living room. When I asked where to dispose of some used-up napkins, the answer was to drop them right there on the floor. In my travels, I'd learned that such was often the normal state of affairs in lived-in pre-modern dwellings. On one wall the occupants had scribbled family members' cell phone numbers on the plaster. On another hung a chart of Chinese characters meant to help kindergarteners learn to read. The chart showed medieval poems, albeit with phonetic aids, that the children were expected to memorize, many of the same ones that I had memorized as a kid. Running water came through a hose in the yard, but when we asked to wash our hands, a basin was brought out and its water poured over our palms onto the concrete steps.

From the farmhouse we walked out through the fields, past the farmers sweating in the sun, their torsos tanned chocolate, toward a row of tombstones. Under one of these lay my grandfather. My father and uncle had erected the stone when they brought his ashes here, back to his once and forever home.

Next to his was the tombstone of the only other relative who went with him to Taiwan, who had also died there, and whose ashes had also been brought back as though to keep my grandfather eternal company. This "uncle," I learned, was forced to leave home because he had been a prison guard, and a murderer escaped under his watch.

"He was responsible, you know," Pingsheng explained, "and he could have been punished very severely for letting the prisoner get away." Instead he chose to take his chances with my grandfather.

My grandfather's story was much more common for the times if no less dramatic: a patriotic young man, in fact a teenager, left home to enlist in the army when war with Japan began. In truth, his story had seemed so commonplace to me that I had previously missed the drama in it. My maternal grandfather had done the same. By the end of this day, however, I would come to see the story in a new light.

My cousins lit the incense sticks and handed them to me. I did as I was supposed to, knelt down before my grandfather's grave and bowed repeatedly. I was also supposed to pray to him in some way, but I'd never been a praying man and couldn't think of anything to say. Ashley, bewildered by the strange ritual but trying to be a good sport, knelt down next to me, which she was really only meant to do if we were married.

Then my cousins set the paper money on fire. The belief was that by burning it, the "money" would transfer to the underworld into the account of the deceased person it was meant for. Of course it was an absolutely ridiculous notion that offended my skeptical, scientific sensibilities: Where do I start? The idea that dead souls in Hades still need cash? That they had bank accounts down there like J.P. Morgan Chase? That random pieces of paper that some guy in a shop scribbled numbers on constituted money? That burning things sent them to the underworld? What next, Bitcoin for the dead?

But it was tradition, so I kept my thoughts to myself. Then one cousin lit up the firecrackers, which burned and burst dangerously before the tombstones. The explosive reports, loud enough to make me jump, echoed even against the trees.

We moved to the next set of tombstones and repeated the exercise of wasting paper and producing gratuitous air pollution. But one pair of gravestones caught my eye. They were the same modest size and stood side by side, and the carvings on both were crude like a child's scrawl. Or more accurately, like the family, unable to find or to pay a mason, took a chisel and carved the stones themselves.

In fact, that was what they had done. When I asked him about these tombstones and our relatives interred beneath, Pingsheng turned to me with downcast eyes.

"They died before reform began," he said quietly, referring to the policy changes made after Mao's death. That was explanation enough.

I checked the dates on the tombstones: 1977 and 1979.

On the outskirts of Han Bay, I saw one more tombstone of one more relative. This one had the word "martyr" carved on it.

"Why was he a martyr?" I asked my cousin.

"He died resisting the Japanese during the war," Pingsheng explained. "Had he lived — they said he was just as talented as your grandfather and could have been so much more had he only lived."

I had never thought of my grandfather as particularly talented. But perhaps it was another case of familiarity breeding contempt. Measured by the standards of rural China in the 1930s, he must have seemed a bright scion, the vessel of the family's hopes.

Returning to the farmhouse, my relatives served a home-cooked dinner. A feast, really. The mud fish in the pot, they said, was caught right in the river outside.

"Careful now," an "aunt" said as she placed a piece of fish in my bowl, "it's bony." River fish often are.

My cousins poured beer for everyone who did not refuse, and periodically someone would raise a glass to drink to me or to another relative. Another custom — instead of involving the entire table in a general "cheers" or making a toast, at a Chinese table one asks to clink glasses with a specific individual. This was typically how a guest of honor wound up under the table. Several such honors came my way.

They showed me the family tree. The tradition was to update and reprint the book once every couple of generations, and my father had been involved in putting together the latest edition. I read with interest the recent entry about me, which told posterity that I studied at "a university in New York." Then I read the entries about my father and grandfather and my great-grandfather, the lawyer I never knew.

Each entry referred to the previous ancestor, so that from my great-grandfather I could find my great-great-grandfather and so on all the way to the clan's founding in 1371. According to the book, I was of the nineteenth generation. I began tracing backward one generation at a time. But precise dates were only available up to the tenth generation. My patrilineal ancestor in that position in the lineage was born in 1649 and died in 1723. Any earlier than that and the names became detached from chronology and felt lost in myth. I lingered over these pages under the curious gaze of my gaggle of kinsmen.

These pages seemed to me a record almost exclusively of the unremarkable lives of unremarkable men. (Chinese genealogies primarily recorded men.) Particular accomplishments, as with my great-grandfather, were reflected here if only in the briefest summary. But the pages were silent with respect to most of them. These were lives that began at a certain time, say 1649, and ended at another time, say 1723, with seemingly nothing noteworthy happening in the span of those decades.

They were born, they lived, they procreated, and they died. Mostly within a ten-mile radius of this farmhouse. If ever they tossed in the cards that life dealt them and demanded a new hand, if ever they stood atop a tall tower and sounded the barbaric yawp, if ever they staked their ground and made themselves more than they were, then these pages failed to record how.

We are not the descendants of emperors and generals and poets and philosophers. Maybe some people are, but not us. Instead, most of my ancestors tilled the land to eke out a living.

And yet I am not descended from fearful men. When the time came, my grandfather left home at seventeen to fight for his country, while his less courageous brothers stayed behind to carve tombstones for their own family. So, too, my maternal grandfather marched off the farm at nineteen and fought in two consecutive wars. And my maternal grandmother as well, who ran from an abusive stepmother at fifteen to enlist and rose to an officer's rank in a man's army.

Even in times of peace, we can't leave well enough alone. My great-grandfather, who decided that he was better than a life tilling the land and became a lawyer and businessman. My parents, who left behind the life that they used to know to move to a strange land on the far side of the earth, where people spoke an alien language and would never accept them entirely.

And me.

We are the people who get up and leave. We are the people who hike over the next foothill just to see what is there. We are the people who don't sit still. We are the people who would have lives less ordinary. My grandparents, who migrated in wartime, crossed frontiers out of necessity and patriotism, but also because they already had the wandering spirit in them, when others in their families did not. And their journeys transformed them, as journeys do.

We are not that strength which in old days moved earth and heaven, because even in the old days we never were. But we are those always roaming with a hungry heart.

Gan Ying might well have come from a village like this one and been born in a farmhouse like this one. He, too, would have left behind the path seemingly ordained for him. He went to serve his country and to seek the life of a soldier and adventurer. Eventually he would pursue the final frontier of his time, a semi-mythical country at the far end of the earth. And like Gan

Ying, perhaps, we are to varying degrees explorers of a sort. Our natural condition is dissatisfaction.

Ashley sat demurely beside me through all this, not entirely following what was going on. My relatives were in turn solicitous of the pale blonde in the black dress who seemed incongruously fashionable relative to the surroundings. Solicitous and gingerly. A mosquito bit her on the leg, and they looked terribly ashamed and began fussing about with insect-repellent incense.

I asked them when the last time was that a foreigner had visited the village. "Last time?" they ruminated. "Last time would be the Japanese soldiers, during the war."

I laughed. "Perhaps we ought not to count an invading army," I said. "So, setting aside the war, when was the time before that?"

"Before that, in the 1800s, there were some French missionaries who built a church nearby. Actually the church is still there."

I left the farmhouse that afternoon feeling superior for not being my cousins. Something set my branch of the family apart, I decided. My grandparents on both sides had the courage to leave home and risk it all to join the fray. Their siblings remained and played it safe only in the end to suffer, and to make their children suffer, the consequences of their timidity. Let us be like sharks and keep moving forward.

*****

Given my smugness, of course my cousin and his wife immediately put me in my place. My parents had given me the impression that old ways of hospitality might have died away in these parts of the Mainland. They even led me to think that perhaps a local Communist Party cadre would ask to meet me to assess my espionage potential. I was doubtful of the apparatchik meeting but willing to believe that the tradition of hospitality was not what it used to be. I was mistaken.

The following day, Pingsheng and his wife drove me and Ashley westward to the mountains of Zhangjiajie, where I would take a bit more time before further pursuing Gan Ying's footsteps. It took almost the entire day to get there, a fact that distressed me as I castigated myself for accepting Pingsheng's offer to drive us. He was taking another day off work, having taken off the previous day to bring us to Han Bay. And given the distance, I wondered when they would be able to get home.

"No worries, Brother," he said to me, having noticed me squirm. "I'm a professional driver. We have ways of staying awake through long hours on the road."

Silently, I hoped that he was right.

As we parted ways, my cousin's wife took a red envelope out of her purse and stuffed it in my hands. Surprised — I had meant to pay him to compensate for a day's lost earnings — I protested that I could not possibly accept. But of course in that inimitable way of the Chinese, she refused to take back the envelope and in the end left me with it. When I opened it, I found the equivalent of over a thousand U.S. dollars.

This from a cab driver and his wife. In a country where the median annual income was still only a few thousand dollars. I asked myself whether, if a cousin I had never met showed up at my door and implicitly demanded that I drive him around for two straight days, I would hand him a thousand dollars on his way out. The answer was an emphatic "no." Much to my embarrassment, over and over they had proclaimed me a man of "high culture," in supposed contrast to themselves. Yet here they displayed a level of culture that I could never match. My parents were entirely mistaken. Traditional Chinese hospitality, in which men and women would go beyond their means and to embarrassing lengths for the sake of a guest, remained as frustratingly entrenched as ever. It was a creature not easily killed. Not years of war, not famines, not communism, not capitalism, could put an end to it.

This, then, must also enter into the case file of the mystery of China.

*****

Zhangjiajie — literally "the Zhang family's boundary" — is a forest both of stones and of trees. Hundreds of karst formations, those sublime mountainscapes somehow bearing the unmistakable stamp of Asia, shot up from the ground hundreds of feet into the air. These austere shapes, more rectangular than triangular as we normally imagine mountains, gave the impression of restraint and self-denial, true Asian values.

Pines twisted like over-sized bonsais struggled out of the crags where thin layers of dirt had gathered over eons, as though bursting forth out of the rocks themselves, gesturing expectantly toward the sun. Take a close look at them, and Chinese landscape paintings with their abstract brushwork and uncertain perspectives suddenly make much more sense. Indeed, that image of a tree growing sideways out of the ruthless face of a rock is no less than a statement of Chinese moral philosophy.

I harbored naive illusions that I would find some measure of peace amidst those rocks and trees. I should have known better, having climbed famous mountains in China before. But still the opposite of peace took me by bitter surprise.

Men, women, and children jostling each other on narrow mountain passes. Tour guides waving flags on long thin aluminum staffs. Tourists waving selfie sticks like swords of narcissism. Tourists carrying little speakers on their persons so that their personal soundtracks accompanied them through the forest, lest they fall victim to the quietude of nature. Touts and shopkeepers constantly asking whether you wanted to eat or to buy whatever. Touts selling selfie sticks on mountaintops just in case you forgot to bring you own, and no one forgot. Tourists in groups of dozens relying on tour guides to tell them when they could go to the bathroom. Tour guides and touts and shopkeepers together speaking through megaphones so that they could be heard through the din of hundreds and thousands of people playing their personal soundtracks, thereby amplifying the cacophony so much more.

Lines formed around wooden stockades for this cable car or this bus or that elevator (they had built one into the side of a mountain) so that the tourists, Chinese for once forced to line up, resembled cattle in pens. And when the vehicle or contraption in question arrived, they broke into a mad dash, elbowing each other out of the way, like contestants in some peculiarly inhumane form of animal racing.

And the powers-that-be of local tourism had given every last rock in the area a fancy name, so that the maps of the area they gave out were covered in tiny print. Like Adam in the Garden of Eden, the Chinese liked to declare their dominion over nature by naming everything. What it meant now was that, at every stop, tour guides had a ridiculous story to tell. One more addition to the cacophony.

It was as though the Chinese found a place with peace and quiet and thought, "Can't have that," so they brought the noise with them. They found something pristine and, without perhaps consciously deciding to do so, proceeded to dirty it and bring it down to the level of mundane mud. A day on these sublime mountains was like a day walking endlessly through Grand Central Terminal at rush hour, enough to raise anyone's blood pressure.

And then there was the movie *Avatar*. The Hallelujah Mountains of Pandora were the mountains of Zhangjiajie, except in the James Cameron film they floated midair with the help of CGI. One mountain in the area was now called "Avatar Hallelujah Mountain." Screenshots from the film, blown up and printed on banners and yet fading in the sun and never very clear to begin with due to the cheap reproduction, adorned walls and rock faces here. A life-size sculpture of the alien bird that Sam Worthington's character learns to ride stood atop one peak for tourists to sit on and take pictures with. But the coat of paint over it was chipping away badly, as though out of embarrassment.

Yes, yes, all these Chinese seemed to be saying eagerly, this was the Avatar mountain, this was the rock that an *American* director decided to include in his *American* film, so it must be important and worth seeing. A white man had approved of this thing that they had, and in winning his approval they showed their desperation for it. With much less fanfare, a few signs noted that a recent version of *Journey to the West*, that endlessly re-adapted Ming Dynasty novel featuring the Monkey King, was also filmed there. A couple of despondent men in simian costumes, behind rubber masks that were creepy more than anything else, struck primate poses in order to charge money for pictures. Their shoes, though, were shoddy white sneakers, hardly the footwear of a trickster god.

But then, sometimes, the real monkeys came out of the trees. Sometimes, when you couldn't believe your good luck, you found yourself having miraculously gotten away from the crowing crowds. Sometimes there were no men in weird costumes around or cheap images taken out of Hollywood films. And for a few short minutes you were alone on a mountaintop, amidst the clouds, looking down on stubborn pines stealing through harsh crags in the rocks and reaching for the sky. For a moment you felt the transcendent, and you remembered why you came all the way out here, and you understood why the Chinese imagined gods and immortals perched upon these rocks like blades piercing forth through the earth. For a moment you felt a touch of the divine.

Until suddenly the din of it all caught up with you again.

*****

To travel is to be reminded of your race, to have others define you by what they perceive you to be. Even when they're wrong, their mistakes force you to define yourself, if only in your mind. As a Taiwanese New Zealander living in America, I had grown used to this fact of life, the way the vast majority of human beings refuse their fellows the freedom to define themselves. But still it could get under my skin.

Ashley had never received this kind of attention before. Now people did double takes as she walked by and then a triple take when they realized that she was with me.

"Is... is he Chinese?" A young woman asked out loud regarding me, as Ashley and I passed by, apparently not concerned whether I would hear or understand.

"Nah," said the young man she was with, just as loudly. "Must be Japanese if he's with a foreign girl."

When we stopped for a snack, one young man, a food seller, asked me for advice on dating American women.

"Well," I said, "the first thing you do is, you learn English."

"Aiyah," he waved one hand urgently as though warding off the sudden apparition of an unpleasant ghost. "Forget it, forget it."

At times, kids and adults alike came up to Ashley just to say hello. I mean just to pronounce the English word, "hello." And when she didn't respond they declared her rude in Mandarin. She looked at me helplessly for some hint as to what to do.

It reminded me of my teenage years in New Zealand, when kids would approach me in school and everyday about town just to say "*konichiwa*" (which of course is Japanese, not a language I spoke) or to bow in mocking exaggeration before breaking out in laughter like cartoon hyenas. Perhaps I ought to have fended them off for her. And perhaps I didn't because a not-so-small part of me wanted her to experience what I had experienced for most of my life. Perhaps I thought it would help her understand me better. Or perhaps I was just being cruel.

She, too, had crossed the invisible line of race, if much less consciously and deliberately than I had. And she was paying a price for it, as I had paid a price. Ought I be grateful to that extent?

*****

The tour groups and their guides and flags and touts and loudspeakers followed us to Fenghuang, meaning "Phoenix," a few hours south of Zhangjiajie.

I had two reasons for wanting to make a stop here. One is that Fenghuang was a preserved old town on riverbanks, so ironically rare now in a country so boastful of its ancient history, with a magical and romantic atmosphere.

Secondly, it was the hometown of Shen Congwen, one of the greatest figures of modern Chinese literature. His most famous novel, *Bordertown*, was set in a small and idyllic if unnamed town with a river running through it very much based on Fenghuang. A tragic love story about an elderly ferryman, his granddaughter, and the two brothers who fall in love with her, *Bordertown* was one of the most influential novels written in Chinese in the twentieth century.

Shen's former home had become a museum, its walls lined with black-and-white photos from an age ago. Ah yes, we could all agree now to admire the famous author. But during the Cultural Revolution, Shen the intellectual (never mind that he officially only ever graduated from elementary school) suffered terrible persecution. Working as a janitor during those harrowing years, Shen scrubbed toilets for a living.

Even long after the Cultural Revolution ended, the authorities were hesitant to acknowledge him. In 1988, the Swedish Academy shortlisted Shen for the Nobel Prize in Literature. The Academy contacted the Chinese embassy in Stockholm to inquire about the whereabouts of the great novelist. In response, the embassy claimed that there was no such person. By the time the Swedes finally tracked him down, Shen had died of a heart attack. The Nobel Prize could only be awarded to the living.

As Shen lay on his deathbed, someone prompted him for his last words.

"I have nothing to say to this world," he replied.

In any event, had Shen still been around, he might not have recognized Fenghuang. Its environs remained, but its atmosphere was much changed. No longer a quiet and soulful border town, at night its old wooden buildings, now bars and clubs, lit up in neon signs and strobe lights. Kitschy pop music vibrated hazardously against aged rooflines. Some stereo across the river demanded the patrons to "Jump! Jump! Jump!" Had they all obeyed, there was no telling whether the wooden beams holding them up from the river's muddy water would not have collapsed under the weight of their collective ecstasy.

And then there was the jingoism. One bar had a cartoonish mural on the outside of an angry man in a boat on the sea with a caption proclaiming the disputed Senkaku/Diaoyu Islands to be

Chinese. "Japan hands off," read the caption. Another bar had a sign on its door: "Japanese will not be served here." It should've been another piece of evidence for my case file. But it was another missed clue.

*****

A kind of nostalgia drew me to Chengdu. You might ask how that could be, and you'd have a point: I had never been there before.

Chengdu served as one of the main stages of the Three Kingdoms period. The history of that formative era was already redolent with drama and heroism by the time a 14th-century novelist fictionalized it and made historical figures into popular legends. *The Romance of the Three Kingdoms* was my favorite book as a child. It brightened more than a few dreary afternoons in school when the lessons bored me, and I surreptitiously read it under my desk.

Later I would come to think of the book as a Chinese Iliad. At least the quarter of the novel concerning the Battle of the Red Cliff. The debate among the courtiers over whether to fight parallels the embassy to Achilles. The final stratagem that wins the battle reminds me of the Trojan Horse. And the pantheon of sharply drawn heroes, their courage and foibles equally visible to all, calls to mind the names of not only Achilles and Odysseus but also Ajax and Agamemnon and Menelaus and Nestor and Diomedes and Hector and Helen and Paris and Priam, characters so luminously lit up on the page as though they stood beneath a cloudless Aegean sky.

Both are epics about societies on the verge of collapse, both are about cataclysmic wars, and both are exemplars of that Chinese saying: "In an age of chaos, heroes arise." Both epics went on to inspire further art down through the generations, serving as foundational texts of their respective civilizations. Tennyson's poem is, after all, called "Ulysses."

The Chinese mythologized the Three Kingdoms era, the protracted death throes of the Han Dynasty a century after Gan Ying's journey. Innumerable shrines and temples are dedicated to the heroes of that time, many of them now deified, so large they were supposed to have been in life, and so vast their shadows. And the most significant temple dedicated to them was here in Chengdu.

I went there to indulge in my nostalgia. Carved in the stone walls of the temple grounds first built in 223 A.D. were poems and essays that I had learned as a child and still returned to in moments of reflection. And there they were, my favorite lines from the great strategist Zhuge Liang (imagine an amalgam of Sherlock Holmes, Dr. Strange, and Dwight Eisenhower) to his emperor: "Your servant was but a commoner in cotton clothes, farming in Nanyang. Having been lucky enough to survive in an age of chaos, I harbored no hope of being known to a prince. Yet the late emperor in his mercy condescended thrice to visit me in my thatched hut..." and so on went his third century letter. To me, the letter had always read as a reminder to count my blessings in times of difficulty, be they a global financial crisis or a global pandemic.

From the temple, Ashley and I couldn't find a cab to go back. Rush hour had come, and raindrops the size of beans fell on our heads. A tuk-tuk stopped.

"You want a ride?" asked the paunchy, middle-aged man in his white, sweat-stained undershirt.

I asked Ashley whether it'd be all right. She nodded but with hesitation. When we got back, she stood on the curb, looked at me, shrugged her shoulders and tucked in her chin in a way that was something between sheepish and coquettish, and whispered in confidential baby-talk, "I rode a tuk-tuk today." It was her first time riding one of these motorcycles with little carriages attached that were the common means of conveyance in so many developing countries.

I had to think for a minute to remember my first time riding a tuk-tuk: it was on that early foray into Southeast Asia. She and I were made of different stuff. I fancied myself an adventurer ready to rough it when necessary; she was a delicate princess who enjoyed the finer things. I relished my independence; she liked to hear me say that I would take care of her. I was constant in my skepticism; she once told me that she could not believe that her father, who died when she was a teenager, was not looking down on her from Heaven.

*****

Not far south of Chengdu was the town of Leshan, or "Happy Mountain." It was now the site of the world's largest outdoor Buddha statue, now that the Taliban had blown up the massive Buddha statues of Bamiyan. I hoped to visit Bamiyan when I reached Afghanistan to see the empty, melancholy niches where the serene figures once stood. So first I had to see the replacement batter.

Another reason for my visit was that this was where my maternal grandparents met. It was in the middle of World War II. Much of what remained of China's government and military, besides professors from all her universities, retreated to this province, Sichuan, about as far away from Japanese bombers as they could get without ending up in another country.

Both of my grandparents, having left home as teenagers to join the war effort, wound up in the area. My grandmother had gotten kicked out of her unit because a superior officer read her personal diary and found that she had called him names in those pages. Now she drifted to Leshan. Then a malarial mosquito bit her and kept her in bed for two months.

My grandfather heard about her through a friend from the military academy. He decided, sight unseen, that she was the one for him, and began writing love letters to her. She ignored him until one final letter came. It explained that he had been assigned to the expeditionary army to Burma to relieve the beleaguered British, and he would soon ship out. This was a suicide mission, so my grandmother agreed finally to meet with the young man on his way to die. Luckily for them and for me, his orders subsequently changed, but not before they had their first date on the dock in Leshan.

(Years later in Taiwan, my grandfather's mentor and a commander on the Burma expedition, General Sun Liren, American-educated and nicknamed "Rommel of the East," was accused of conspiring with the CIA to take power. Whatever coup attempt there might have been, my grandfather was never involved. Nonetheless, Colonel Yin was a known associate of General Sun. His military career came to an abrupt end. So that was the time when the CIA altered my family's fate. But who's keeping score?)

Here in Leshan, in front of the 1,200-year-old stone Buddha, three rivers converged in a riparian dance that had been going on since long before even the Wise One was conceived in the sculptor's mind. Two muddy and one clear, the waters mixed uneasily like an ill-advised cocktail.

When the artisans started carving this colossal figure into the cliff face in the seventh century, the Tang Dynasty was at the height of its power, the grandest empire on earth. By the time they were done, in 803 A.D., the empire was in steep decline.

35

Defeat by Muslim forces in the Battle of Talas in today's Kyrgyzstan, in 751, was the pinprick that burst the balloon. By 755, a cataclysmic rebellion cut a swath of desolation through the country, making a refugee of the emperor himself and killing two-thirds of the Chinese empire's population.

The Great Buddha of Leshan watched this decline and fall and all the declines and falls that were yet to come, all the cruelty and barbarism, all the bodies writhing in agony and faces contorted with pain, with the same serenity that he wears even now. One wondered how he could be so indifferent. But it was only a thin line between indifference and Zen.

And then I remembered his Afghan brethren, lost to history as one of humanity's many follies destroyed one of humanity's many accomplishments, and remembered that he would be equally indifferent or Zen to their destruction, as they would have been to their own. Enlightenment means seeing through the impermanence of all things, not least oneself.

And, I supposed, crimes were no more and no less likely to go unpunished in China than in Afghanistan.

In the mountain around the colossal figure, Han Dynasty tombs abounded. Hillside caves with stone coffins and urns and bas reliefs depicting horses and horsemen, kings and assassins, figures so lively and with such dynamism that they would not have seemed out of place in Periclean Athens or Renaissance Florence. These people buried here were Gan Ying's contemporaries. Perhaps they, too, had heard rumors of a country called Rome. Perhaps they had read the news of his departure and some years later his return.

*****

Chengdu was as far as Ashley would accompany me. She was

36

heading back to New York.

We had drinks at the Wide and Narrow Alleys, an old part of town where imperial troops were once quartered, now fixed up with bars and restaurants. In the summer heat, the condensation on the outside of our emerald Tsingtao beer bottles dripped like beads of sweat. Crowds passed us by, their din becoming our background.

I contemplated her across the table. After all this time, I still wasn't sure how to think of her. She peered back at me with her big gray eyes, questioning.

Was she the innocent princess who called on me to protect her? That was a role that she played, surely. A role that she enjoyed playing in light of the early death of her father.

Was she the buxom temptress who wanted to have me—and other men—wrapped around her little finger? That was also a role she played, though one that she played without conviction.

I had arranged the car to take her to the airport in the morning. Now that the logistics were taken care of, I found that I could think of nothing more to say about her pending departure. The same, it seemed, could be said for her.

I remembered my Nietzsche: that we find words for what is already dead in our hearts; there is necessarily a kind of contempt in the act of speaking.

"Hey," I began to speak. "What do you think? I mean about us…"

"Shh…" She pressed a finger against her lips.

We finished our drinks.

"You want to go?" I asked.

"Okay."

We went back to our hotel. Got undressed. Showered.

"Come to bed," she said.

I did as I was told.

The next morning, she flew out.

That was the last time I ever saw her. That was the end of the story of me and Ashley, the captain's daughter.

*****

More Nietzsche: To live alone, one must be an animal or a god, said Aristotle. Nietzsche added a third possibility — a philosopher. I felt like none of the above.

But no matter. Now I was alone, a man set loose into the world. Now the game could truly be afoot. It was time to head to the eastern stretches of the Silk Road.

Jiayuguan was the western terminus of the Great Wall ("guan" meaning "pass" or "gate"). The mouth of China, as some liked to say. But the Great Wall is like the Ship of Theseus. True, the original Wall was built under the First Emperor in 200-something B.C., and some of the fortresses dated back even further. But over the centuries, it was built and rebuilt and renovated and demolished and extended and truncated many times. Whether it was all the same Wall is a question of metaphysics. The Jiayuguan Fortress as it stood now was built in 1372, during the Ming Dynasty. It would not have been where Gan Ying exited into the unknown.

In Gan Ying's day, the Wall stretched much farther west to the ancient kingdom of Qiuci or Kuche in today's Xinjiang. In the first century B.C., Wudi of the Han, "the Martial Emperor," extended the Wall westward by hundreds of miles to reach this, the farthest outpost of the Empire. The Great Wall marked territory, ostensibly to keep invaders out, but also to keep citizens in, or at least their imagination and worldview, just like the Great Firewall of today that controlled China's Internet and kept out Western viewpoints. As military strategy, the Wall was hopelessly static. As a symbol, it represented a desperate desire to control and to keep things just so.

It would have been there that Gan Ying bade his country farewell. But that section of the Wall was by now no more than a few eroded rocks in the desert. I had plans to go out to Kuche anyway, but Jiayuguan was potentially an ahistorical but more evocative illustration of what it might have been like for Gan Ying to reach the end of the Great Wall, to turn around and see his country behind him, and to keep going into the unknown. To leave behind all that was familiar.

It must have been frightening for any Chinese to go past the enclosure. As far as they knew, civilization existed on their side of the divide. Beyond it lay barbarism and who knew what monsters. How might Gan Ying have felt, watching his homeland fade away behind him? But Gan Ying was no ordinary man. He was a decorated veteran of the Hunnic war and one of Ban Chao's thirty-six commandos.

Jiayuguan Fortress as it stood was unfortunately heavily and all-too-obviously reconstructed. When Paul Theroux passed through here in the late 1980s, he described the Great Wall here as "a crumbled pile of mud bricks and ruined turrets that the wind had simplified and sucked smooth... the remnants of a great scheme." Not anymore. Now the bricks and turrets looked almost new enough to form a part of some rich guy's Malibu McMansion and with almost as little soul. I certainly would have preferred that authentic desolation that Theroux spoke of, the romantically derelict.

What the fortress offered now was primarily its dramatic setting against the Qilian Mountains, snowy even in July like the head of a bald eagle. When Wudi's armies defeated the Huns on an earlier occasion, the nomadic people sang: "You take the Qilian Mountains from us, and our cattle have no place to graze. You take the Yanzhi Mountains from us, and our women have no rouge to paint their faces." While they lamented beyond the Wall, within it, the Han rejoiced. Change the scene from the first century B.C. to the second decade of the twenty-first century, and much remained the same.

All around, the landscape was that of a proto-desert, prelude to the bitter expanse of sand stretching westward that dared explorers and settlers alike to enter here and abandon what hope they had. But from atop the fortress, between the crenellations where archers would have shot at invaders beneath, one could see the modern power plant not so far away, its urn-shaped chimneys, four of them, encroaching on the ancient site as Hunnic horsemen might have seemed to defenders within.

I found a better setting for picturing how things might have looked to Gan Ying as he departed at another nearby section of the Wall, described as "hanging" or "cantilevering." More recent than the rest — built in the mid-16th century — it was more authentically preserved. I hiked up to the topmost watchtower, and, out of breath, looked around where I was. The shoddy modernity was still there, right there below the rocky hills, past the trees that General Tso (or in modern romanization, Zuo), he of the chicken fame, planted when he came here to put down the 19th century Muslim rebellion. (History really does repeat itself.) But if I only stuck out my thumb at the correct angle and blotted out the new concrete city, what surrounded me felt like true desolation.

Below this section of the Wall, two more modern intrusions confronted me. One was a concrete train of camels with figures meant to resemble Persian traders, their clothes painted in gaudy colors, representing the Silk Road. The other was a sculptural group, carved in a less than tasteful and less than skillful variation on Socialist Realism, representing major historical figures who made their marks along this famous route.

Here was Marco Polo. The stone tablet under his figure credited him with everything he claimed he did in his *Travels*, despite scholarly doubts. Another figure was Ban Chao. A third was Zhang Qian, the first great Chinese explorer to head westward and Gan Ying's great predecessor. In 138 B.C. Wudi sent Zhang on a secret and hazardous mission through this area then under the Huns' control to reach the nation known as the Yuezhi in Transoxiana. Zhang returned after thirteen years (including ten spent in Hun captivity) to report on the western nations that he encountered or learned about. It was likely from this report that the Chinese first heard of Rome.

Gan Ying himself, though, was nowhere to be found.

I left the Wall to return to the modern town of Jiayuguan. Once the lonely outpost on the desert's edge, it now seemed so typical of smaller towns in China, a collection of mostly single-story ramshackle buildings pressed together as though by an inattentive pupil for a silly school assignment.

At least unlike in major cities, no oddly proportioned near-replicas of the Chrysler or the Empire State Buildings loomed over the cityscape like grotesque giants. Only an abstractly ugly metallic sculpture rose high over a traffic circle overlooking the city's arteries. But at least it wasn't another statue of Mao; so many of those plaster ogres stood in the middle of town squares all over China, invariably poorly sculpted as though by an artists' vengeful compact against a man who destroyed art. Along the streets, restaurants and grocery stores and bike dealerships and mechanics' workshops kept their lights off during the day, leaving their establishments looking gloomy and alternately sinister or unhygienic. On a lazy Saturday afternoon, the proprietors fell asleep in bamboo chairs by the doors.

*****

Such a ramshackle place I was happy to leave behind. I took the train headed toward Kuche by the Tarim Basin, deep inside Xinjiang.

Getting there required a twenty-four-hour train ride with a transfer in Urumqi, the provincial capital. I found my berth in the sleeper car. A woman was sleeping on it, the railway-issued pillow and comforter, pale blue with a strangely childish pattern of stars and hearts, all screwed up beneath her with the signs of human habitation and excretion.

Foolishly I had expected a fresh train, but the train had come all the way from Manchuria, thousands of miles away to the east. One could only imagine how many passengers had gotten on and off and how many bodies had slept in these berths by now. A man in the next compartment half bragged to somebody that it had taken three days and three nights to get here.

"This is car number eight, compartment ten, yes?" I asked just to be sure.

"Yes," the woman's companion, another middle-aged woman, allowed with a frown that this was my berth by right. "Come on, let's move." The sleeping woman reluctantly vacated her/my space, leaving me to excavate bits of her hair from the sheets.

They turned out to be members of a family spread out over several compartments but sadly centered in mine. The young children above me were theirs. Another sister-in-law and their husbands came and went. The children (all four of them, two boys and two girls) screamed and cried and spilled tea on their clothes. The youngest, a boy, wore a pair of *kaidangku*, that age-old but lazy Chinese solution to potty training, where the pants are cut open in the crotch, exposing the buttocks and genitalia. This was so that when a boy shat his pants, he wouldn't actually shit his pants but soil the floor. Obviously, this was only a solution to potty training if the floor was someone else's problem. The kid rolled around in his berth, waving his schlong in my face. The family was going to visit the children's grandfather. I watched the adults eat instant noodles and play cards and hit their children.

As soon as I ceased to take up the entire length of my berth, one or another family member claimed the space by adverse possession. A father would sit down, or a child. A mother would push away my bedding to make more space for the child, and the child would push me aside to make space for herself. They did all of this without embarrassment or apology. There are too many people in China, and as a mathematical necessity personal spaces shrink to vanishing. Hannah Arendt once postulated that a sense of privacy and private space was essential to democracy, because only after we develop our ideas in private can we exchange them in public. If Arendt was right, and I think she was, then the sheer population density worked against any potential democratization in this country.

The last time I took a long-distance train like this I was a dozen years younger and in college. It was the Trans-Siberian Railroad followed by further train journeys in China. I now had the distinct and forlorn feeling that I was growing too old for this kind of travel.

Meanwhile the desert landscape rolled by outside, a bleak panorama. Stern and scruffy clumps of grass grew amidst the sands and stones. A sign of life, yes, but it also robbed the desert of its arid majesty, as though it somehow lacked commitment in its own being. Cowardice is an unattractive quality in nature as it is in people. An hour out the train passed by a wind farm, and some hours later another, and another, and another. Arrays of slender, white wind turbines, armies of Don Quixote's giants after an aggressive weight loss program. Modern renewable energy technology standing in the middle of the same sand and pebbles that likely saw Gan Ying pass through here nearly two thousand years ago.

The hours began to pass, as they do on long train journeys, with a kind of lethargic impatience, passing more quickly than one might expect and yet feeling slower than one imagined. Until, finally, I arrived at the scene of the crime.

*****

"Xinjiang" in Chinese means "new border territory." The Uyghurs, the Turkic-speaking Muslim people who once formed the majority population in the region, traditionally called it "East Turkestan." China dominated much of the area in the Han (201 B.C. – 220 A.D.) and Tang (618 – 906 A.D.) dynasties, but not in the long periods in between. Then in the 17th and 18th centuries, the Qing Dynasty (1644 – 1911), run by the Manchu people, conquered it again after prolonged military engagements. It was the Manchu emperors who began calling the area "New Territory." It was a similar picture with Tibet – it was the Manchus who brought that theocracy within the folds of their empire. To most Chinese now, the very idea that East Turkestan might be its own country is utterly anathema. To them, the minority races should be quaint and cute, good for a night of ethnic singing and dancing but not to be thought about too seriously. And why anyone would not want to be part of the great and mighty Motherland strikes them as an impossible puzzle. Surely it is always better to be part of a big country, they will say, and few countries are bigger than China.

*****

The clumps of dusty weeds now alternated with red Martian

44

deserts as though burnt with fire and the occasional green pastures created and irrigated by human industry. Six hours after departure, the train pulled into the town of Hami, the first stop in Xinjiang. Sweet melons in Chinese are called "Hami melons," referring to this town as the supposed origin of these fruits. Looking at it, though, did not make one think of sweetness or fruits. Construction cranes hovered over sad concrete blocks. For the first time on this journey I saw signs in Arabic script — the alphabet of the Uyghur language — alongside Chinese characters. An implicit announcement of where I was, the culture and people whose home I was entering.

At Turfan (or Turpan or Tulufan), Muslim women in beautiful blue and purple headscarves disembarked with their suitcases. Outside of town stood the Flaming Mountains. The name was a reference to Turfan's heat, but the mountain range in fact resembled in shape and color the flames of a roaring fire. The Ming era novel, *The Journey to the West*, relating the Tang Dynasty monk Xuan Zang's mission to India under the protection of the Monkey King, features these mountains prominently. You could see the novelist's inspiration looking at the jagged peaks. It might have been a novel, but Xuan Zang was very real and one of Gan Ying's major successors as a Silk Road explorer.

We pulled into the regional capital, Urumqi, around seven in the evening. Actually, it was only seven in Beijing, which meant that local time so far west was closer to five, and it was perfectly bright outside. But the government in its infinitely risible wisdom decreed that all of China, from the North Korean border to the foothills of the Himalayas, had to live within one time zone. In the distance, the snowy mountain that loomed was now Tian Shan, the "Heavenly Mountains," a range that stretched from here all the way into the Central Asian republics.

Urumqi South Station was under strict control. Three separate security checkpoints awaited each person who even tried to enter the building: an X-ray scan, a pat-down, and an ID check. A dozen policemen, some Han and some Uyghur, all armed with assault rifles, stood guard directly in front of the station, behind a steel mesh enclosure. An armored police van was parked to the side, fifty meters away. A few more cops with assault rifles stood around the vehicle. The young officer in the driver's seat was, however, asleep.

I fought my way through the crowd to find my next train to Kuche. It arrived at a little before six in the morning, or really four in the morning local time. Cassiopeia was high over my head, in this cloudless clime and starry sky. The city would not truly get started until ten or eleven.

Kuche, or Kuqa, or Qiuci by ancient phonology, or Kucina in Sanskrit, was an independent kingdom that from time to time came under the suzerainty of greater powers, including China. The local people in ancient times were Indo-European. In 91 A.D., after General Ban Chao "pacified the west" and brought dozens of kingdoms under Chinese sway, he made Qiuci the headquarters of his new military "Protectorate."

This place then became the final Chinese outpost before a traveler entered the great beyond. One imagined Gan Ying saying his final goodbyes, cups of rice wine poured and drunk atop a fortress behind battlements, and poetic farewells delivered with the flair of Confucian scholars in flowing robes. Some of the best poems in Chinese literature were written as farewell letters. Ban Chao himself must have been there to wish his protégé good luck and Godspeed.

Whatever the scene might have been back in 97 A.D., little remained now of the Han fortress. Indeed, in the thousand miles between Jiayuguan and here, barely anything of the Great Wall, once greater, still remained. In Kuche itself, near the local mosque, one big yellow rock, worn by the vicissitudes of elements as well as time so as barely to show its origin, stood behind puny white modern railings a few inches off the ground. Something so pathetic meant to protect something once so mighty, and still colossal in scale. An aged warrior, with a craggy face and untold wounds in his torso, arthritis in his joints, but still harboring in his being a strength of spirit not to be trifled with. Another section of the old city wall now formed the outer limits of a parking lot on one side and the boundary of a private yard on another. Look on my works, ye mighty, and despair.

The lone and level sands stretched some miles out of town, where a Han era watchtower still stood. Back then, soldiers on the watchtower would send up a smoke signal when they saw an incoming threat, if during the day, and a fire signal if during the night. It, too, was now no more than two vast and trunkless legs of stone, or rather of dirt, with the remnants of a few wooden beams still atop the structure. Bleak and rocky hillocks and a dried riverbed kept the tower company. One imagined soldiers back then cursing their bad luck when assigned to this lonely outpost amidst nothingness.

This was the Taklamakan Desert, the sort of place where, as the Chinese saying goes, "even the birds don't shit." Its name, one theory goes, means in Turkic "the place of ruins." An alternative etymology says it means "a place of no return," or "once you go in, you don't get out." The Swedish adventurer Sven Hedin, who crossed the Taklamakan, described it as "the worst and most dangerous desert in the world." Sand dunes within reputedly reached as high as three hundred feet. The sun bore down on the traveler from lands antique and modern alike, making him question his sanity and compromising it. Gan Ying would have passed under one of these towers, and another, and another, until he had gotten used to seeing them, and then there were no more, because he had passed beyond the final marker of his civilization. Past this point he would have had nothing but his own knowledge and ability to rely on to get through the remaining length of the world.

*****

I, too, was alone now. But just then I found some unexpected company.

Ms. An had driven me out here. She was in her thirties and from Manchuria in China's northeast. She had moved here six years earlier when her employer, a state-own fertilizer company, reassigned her. In her spare time, she drove tourists around for extra cash. She was far too fashionably dressed for this task in a long blue dress and high heels as well as sleeves to shield her arms from the sun: traditional Chinese notions of beauty abhorred a tan. In sum, she looked like she were headed to a smoke-filled bar and expecting a handsomely craggy gentleman in a slightly rumpled suit to sidle up and ask if he could buy her a whiskey highball.

"You are Chinese, yes?" She had asked me when I hired her.

"That's the way it's turned out," I replied. She laughed. I got into the car.

"So," I asked as we drove down the desert road. "Trouble with the Uyghurs?"

"It's perfectly safe here," her face contorted in a surely unintentional manner as she said this.

That wasn't what I asked.

"The media make everything seem so awful," she went on. "They blow every little incident out of proportion."

"The cops sure looked pretty nervous in Urumqi."

"The local officials," she said, "the provincial party secretaries, the municipal ones, they can't afford even one violent incident on their records. One black mark, and poof!" She took one hand off the wheel, made it into a fist, then exploded it beneath the rearview mirror as illustration. "Careers down the toilet. So any little sign of trouble, and they bring out the guns."

Outside a shuttered mosque, we came upon a pair of young backpackers. The boy was white, the girl Asian.

"All right if I invite them along?" I asked Ms. An. "And split the cost?"

"You can speak English?" she looked at me curiously.

"When necessary."

The elfin-faced, ectomorphic young man turned out to be Theo, a new graduate of Oberlin teaching English in the boondocks of Shanxi Province. He was looking gaunt after a year in China. The young woman was one of his students, a homely and bespectacled girl with a tan. She called herself Rachel. They got into the backseats, and we carried on.

Checkpoint after checkpoint along the highway. Signs and slogans abounded reminding everyone that public displays of faith were "strictly forbidden." It didn't need to be said that they didn't mean Buddhism or Daoism. At each checkpoint, we got out to walk through metal detectors and to present our IDs. I had an Iranian visa stamp in my passport with its flowing Persian script. When I showed my passport at one checkpoint, the officer behind the glass pane tightened up suddenly and struggled mightily against the urge to press the panic button.

"What's with this Muslim stuff?" she demanded.

I put on an exaggerated grin and refocused her attention on the biographical page, trying to remind her that I was as Han as anyone else.

"You should date my niece," Ms. An said to me when we got back into the car after the latest checkpoint.

"How do you figure that?"

"You can speak English," she waved vaguely at Theo. "My niece, she spent four years studying in America. Now that she's back in Beijing she won't go out with anyone who's not either foreign or spent time abroad."

I grunted noncommittally.

Ms. An went on. "She's so picky, won't even go out with guys who make half a million yuan a year." That would be about $80,000. "Here, give me your cell number, so I can give it to her."

I changed the subject.

Theo actually spoke very impressive Mandarin for a young white American, and our conversations were in a mixture of both languages. Over lunch we traded Tang poetry. He wore a question mark on his forehead, as it were, mystified by life and what he ought to do with it. He asked me for advice.

"Hell, kid," I said as I put down my beer. "You think I know?"

*****

Farther away from town, and a little after Gan Ying's time, ancient Kuche artisans carved and painted hundreds of grottoes with Buddhist motifs in what were now called the Kizil Caves. But most of the murals had been defaced.

Muslims riding through this area after the Islamic conquest of the eighth century were eager to tear down any idolatry in sight. But the more significant damages were courtesy of the wine merchant turned archaeologist Albert von Le Coq of Germany, who sawed away entire murals and sculptures from this and other sites to ship back to Berlin only to have a large portion of them destroyed in Allied bombings during World War II.

But Peter Hopkirk's *Foreign Devils on the Silk Road* paints a sympathetic portrait of the man and notes the fraction of Le

Coq's finds that survived. And he was hardly alone—Sven Hedin of Sweden, Aurel Stein of Britain, Langdon Warner of the U.S., Paul Pelliot of France, and Kozui Otani of Japan all came treasure-hunting in and around the Taklamakan. In the process, they contributed to our understanding of this mysterious corner of the world. Le Coq's finds were simply unluckier than the rest.

Le Coq was especially interested in, and wanted to bring back, evidence of European habitation in this part of Asia. So it surprised me to see a representation of the Greek god Apollo on his chariot still intact overhead on the dome of one grotto, to see that Le Coq didn't take this one back to Berlin. But as Hopkirk also notes, Le Coq's senior in the German expedition, Albert Grünwedel, had objected to Le Coq's approach of wholesale removal of art. And with respect to at least one painted dome in the Kizil Caves, Grünwedel had prevailed. Perhaps it was this very dome with the Apollo figure on it.

Also a short distance out of Kuche was the lost city of Subashi. All that remained were some walls and a pagoda of what was once a Buddhist temple. Even so, you could get a sense of the scale of the town that used to stand here. When Xuan Zang passed through here in the seventh century, he recorded a matriarchal country ruled by women whose husbands farmed and fought but held no power. In *Journey to the West*, the novelist portrayed Subashi as instead a country populated entirely by women, the Amazonians of the desert. Likely they were Caucasian women, which would have pleased the German brewer very much.

*****

On the bus to Khotan the driver put on the Uyghur version of American Idol, or "Silk Road Songs."

Not only for Uyghurs either. A young Tajik man came on

wearing a fedora and sang a folk song. And then the strains of a jazz number in English came out of the speakers, and I looked up to find a white American woman on stage in traditional Uyghur clothes. She said her name was Alice Anderson, which sounded suspiciously generic — AA? — but gave a Uyghur name as well. She came from America to study Uyghur language and music. Two of the judges stood up to salute her for making the effort. They wouldn't let her off the stage. Again the eagerness for Western validation. I have wondered since then what might have happened to Alice.

Meanwhile the desert outside began to remind me of the edges of the Sahara that I saw years ago in Egypt. An ocean of sand, boundless, brutal in its purity and pure in its brutality.

Many oasis towns that once ringed the Taklamakan had been lost to the sand over the centuries. Legends abounded since ancient times of biblical sandstorms swallowing up entire cities overnight. Sven Hedin dug up such a city, Loulan, back in 1901. Khotan itself had been buried before and rebuilt. Today's Chinese government planted bands of grass on either side of the highway to control the sand, perhaps twenty-five meters or so into the desert, in lattice patterns like chessboards. It seemed a quixotic enterprise, man's attempt to beat back the inexorable forces of geography. The inhabitants of those lost cities had done what they could as well, to no avail.

Even more than Kuche, Khotan was a heavily Uyghur town, the sort of place where one might not be able to get around speaking Mandarin. It would seem an entirely Central Asian town but for the bilingual street and shop signs. It was the scene of bomb and knife attacks in 2011 and a hijacking in 2012, all attributed by the government to Islamic terrorism.

I took a stroll through the Uyghur night market. Sheep's testicles roasted succulent on a spit. Whiffs of them invaded my nostrils, smoky and gamey. Not one Han Chinese but me was in sight. And the Uyghurs slicing meat with big, menacing knives eyed me suspiciously. Someone clearly foreign would receive a warmer welcome here. I couldn't help looking over my shoulders. Maybe I shouldn't have worried. Maybe I should. Back at the hotel, a large Uyghur man followed me into the elevator with a freshly lit cigarette. He and I exchanged a look. Then he blew smoke in my face.

You might suspect that history here had been cyclical, and you'd be right: Before the Chinese today, Czarist Russia and Britain played their "Great Game" here. Before them, the Islamic and Turkic peoples including the Uyghurs had entered this area and conquered the Buddhist kingdom that once flourished here with the people who spoke a Persian language and had Indian names. These predecessors were the Tocharians, the Indo-European people who also ruled Kuche. They would have been the people that Gan Ying encountered in both areas as he traveled away from Han territory.

I went to my room and sat down at the aged, dented wooden desk to write about the day. A layer of desert dust obscured my window and added to my gloom. Brief glimpses of other rooms as I walked down the corridor did not help. The corridor itself was also miserable. This was, after all, one of those classic old communist hotels, a relic of sadder times.

Overall, modern-day Khotan left me with a sense of futility. Consider the city's efforts at cleaning itself. Given its location amidst a desert, dust perpetually covered everything from beers in the fridge to dashboards in cars. You smacked your lips and realized that you were chewing sand. And yet, in the morning, sanitation workers swept the dust into miniature sand dunes. As soon as the wind blew, the sand dispersed again. It felt like a metaphor for something.

But back in the day, Khotan was the significant oasis of the region. For a time, it was also a center of Buddhism. A monk traveling through Khotan at the end of the fourth century A.D. counted tens of thousands of Buddhist monks and fourteen major monasteries as well as smaller ones. And yet, describing Gan Ying's journey, the *Hou Han Shu* name-checked nearby Pishan instead as a milestone along the southern Silk Road. Given the importance of Khotan at the time, my bet was that Gan Ying passed through both towns. And I would pass through Pishan as well on my way to Kashgar. Modern Pishan turned out to be a miserable collection of factories and residential buildings, some newly built and incongruously candy-colored. They both looked like teenagers dressed for the prom who mysteriously found themselves sitting in a retirement home instead.

*****

Kashgar was the greatest center of Uyghur life as well as the westernmost city in China. As the bird flies, it's closer to Damascus than to Beijing. Only so many reasonable points of egress existed between today's China and post-Soviet Central Asia. The route Marco Polo took, for example, was the Wakhan Corridor, now a lawless section of Afghanistan whose border with China was sealed. So Kashgar would have to serve as my springboard into Central Asia proper.

The overnight bus ride there turned out to be the second worst bus ride I had ever taken by that point—second only to an odyssey from Laos to Vietnam with some guys I figured to be drug smugglers. The vehicle was a double-decker sleeper. The pillow and covers naturally carried an antique accumulation of sweat and grime like a family heirloom. Combined with periodic security checks where everyone had to get off the bus, there could be very little sleep.

At midnight, the bus came to a stop somewhere in the middle of nowhere. The driver needed some shuteye. We stayed there stewing in the patient night heat for three hours. One by one the passengers who couldn't sleep, which was most of us including me, exited the vehicle to escape the suffocation and stood or stooped or sat outside in the dust to wait for the driver to wake up. The stinking public bathroom across the road had no water. Mosquitoes plagued the area. (Mosquitoes in the desert? Who knew?)

Besides me, only three other passengers were Han, and none was foreign. Two were a couple of backpackers from Guangzhou. They were playing Don McLean's "American Pie" on their phone. I considered striking up a conversation to help pass the time, but as I sidled up to the couple, the man let out an uproarious, resonant, declarative fart, without any bourgeois embarrassment or attempt to disguise or apologize for the course of nature. I changed my mind and instead walked in circles around the bus like a Hajji around the Kaaba in Mecca for the next hour.

When we arrived, fourteen hours after departure, the Kashgar station was ghostly in its early morning emptiness. It was technically closed. We ran around knocking on doors and windows to wake up anyone we could find to let us out.

I had been to Kashgar before, some eight years earlier. Even then, the Silk Road already exerted its pull on me. A cloud of dust still hovered menacingly over the city. And I could still sense a kind of pride in the Uyghurs of Kashgar, cognizant as they were that their city was the center of their culture, the uncreated conscience of their race.

But the famed old town was not what it used to be.

A section of the historic town lay to the west of the Idkah Mosque at the town center. But it was far from what I remembered.

Spruced up and commercialized, it had become a grotesque, Disneyland version of itself. The buildings now faced the world with brand new facades. Signs at street corners directed visitors in Chinese, Uyghur, Russian, and Japanese. Here Han Chinese tourists could come and find the ethnic minstrelsy that they liked so much in minority peoples.

The rest of the old town, with its mud thatched roofs and winding streets, lay to the east. This was closer to what I remembered. But barriers now enclosed it like a pen. Demolition seemed only a matter of time. The smell of a threat hung in the air like burned metal.

*****

I knew of two historic hotels in Kashgar, both former consulate buildings, one Russian and one British. I stayed in the Russian one because of a longstanding if conflicted affinity for Russian culture. In college I studied Russian language but never got fluent. And in New York it served as no more than my stand-by parlor trick for impressing former-Soviet emigres at cocktail parties. But it was about to become much more useful.

Seman Hotel's status as a relic of the Great Game came with corresponding decor. Pink and green motifs like Faberge eggs, in the style of the era of perhaps Nicholas II, decorated the walls. The building was in diplomatic service from about 1890 to 1960, when the Sino-Soviet split forced Russian diplomats to return to Moscow. So Czarist aristocrats and their Bolshevik adversaries had both lived and worked here. I imagined Nikolai Petrovsky, the taciturn Russian consul who for three years refused to speak to his British counterpart and opponent, roaming the halls.

All the old splendor had faded by now, like so much that was Russian, that was Russia. Bas-reliefs carved in the plaster walls reminiscent of the culture of St. Petersburg, of the Winter Palace, still looked down upon the weary traveler checking into his room, but the overall impression was that of luxury in decrepitude. A once-beautiful babushka still wearing her pearls and her debutante dress, with poignant effect. And in some respects, the building had been modified to suit Chinese tastes. But one Russian feature remained – a row of copper samovars in the cafeteria, lined up like troops ready for inspection.

I walked through the hotel garden, such as it was, and stumbled on John's Cafe directly behind.

Yes of course, John's Cafe. Memories from eight years ago came back to me. John's was a Xinjiang institution. Back then, all the backpackers in Kashgar made a stop here. I was no exception.

In my memory this was a bustling place, but this time I found it deserted. A young woman slept on her forearms at the cashier's desk. I didn't want to wake her and was about to walk away when John himself came in and woke up his employee. He was a tall and amiable Han Chinese, looking a good decade younger than his years.

"A drink?" John offered. I agreed and we sat down.

"Why 'John's'?" I must have asked the same question eight years ago.

"Easier for foreigners," he said. "They'd never remember Hu Jianjun. Can't even pronounce it."

"I was here some years ago," I volunteered. "I remember it was quite crowded."

"We've had some violent incidents here in Xinjiang." John said by way of explanation. Then he discovered a pack of smokes in his pocket. He took one out and lit it.

"Does it worry you?"

"Not really." John took a long drag of his cigarette. "I will retire next year," he said. "By then I will have run it for thirty years. About time."

It wasn't really John's business prospects I was asking about. But I let it go. "Then?"

"I'm going to drive from here to Europe. Through Kyrgyzstan, Kazakhstan, Turkmenistan, Iran, through former Yugoslavia, all the way to Germany, and then back through Russia. It'll take me five and half months. I have it all planned out."

Everyone wants to travel.

*****

It so happened that Theo of Oberlin had made his way west to Kashgar as well. He sent me the name of his hostel, one of those fleabag places that could be a synecdoche of the romance of youth. I went over just in time to catch his student Rachel leaving in a huff.

"Oh good, you're here," she said bitterly upon seeing me. "You can keep him company." Some lovers' tiff I didn't care to know more about.

Theo and I hired a man to take us to Shipton's Arch. A natural rock formation that made an arch some two hundred and fifty feet high and sixty or seventy feet across, it was originally recorded in the 1940s by Eric Shipton, the last British consul general in Kashgar. Somehow National Geographic had to "rediscover" it in 2000. Both times, obviously, all that anyone had to do to find it was to ask the local villagers: "That mountain with a big hole at the top, where is it?"

Our man was a Uyghur named Tayakuli. He had the mushy midsection and denuded dome of a man well into middle age and didn't care who knew it. He spoke bad Mandarin and worse English. I tried my best to pick up Uyghur words through Turko-Arabic cognates but didn't get too far beyond "merhaba" for hello.

Back in Kashgar I met "Yusup," who ran a tour agency. He was Uyghur, spoke remarkably good English, wrote with beautiful penmanship, and carried himself like a gentleman. He was in his forties with a thin and stringy physique. Deep crow's feet lined the corners of his eyes, which had the effect of emphasizing the benevolence in them. We sat and talked about Xinjiang, past and present. He was the client I never knew I had.

Yusup recalled the Great Game. "Yakub Beg," the Amir of Kashgaria and leader of the Uyghurs, "fought the Russians and then the British and Chinese in this area," in the 19th century. "Then Zuo Zongtang came," that would be General Tso to Americans, "and people say the British helped him as the price of taking Hong Kong" in the Opium War.

"And where are you from?" he asked.

"Taiwan," I said, leaving aside the complicated discussion of my New Zealand upbringing.

"But your English…"

"I've been in living in America."

He nodded with the satisfaction of finding the solution to the puzzle. "Yes, you're very obviously not from around here."

"How's that?"

"I remember a Taiwanese man I met some years back. He took this bus. And he started helping other people with their luggage. The boss of the bus company came out and yelled for him to stop, because the boss was charging money to help people with their luggage. The Taiwan man was very upset. He said he wanted to help."

"And I look like him?"

He laughed. "Something in the mannerisms, in the expression on your face."

But then something clicked in him. "Haven't we met before?" he asked tilting his head sideways.

"I came to Kashgar once eight years ago."

"That's it," he said. "You came into my office to use the Internet." This was before we all had data on our phones, and Internet cafes were still a popular thing.

"My apologies for forgetting," I said.

"That's why I remember," he said, "because you were helpful to a stranger just like that Taiwanese man was. There was another young man, a Westerner, and he was having trouble with some website. You stopped what you were doing to help him. I remember very well because no one around here would drop what they're doing to help a stranger."

What a melancholy statement, I thought, to make about the society in which one lived.

*****

I went out to the Kashgar Sunday livestock market with Theo, an Israeli couple we met along the way, and a young Chinese woman who tagged along. The market was a sight to behold, if only for the immediacy that it brought to humanity's relationship with other animals, which might also represent human beings' relationships to each other, forever stained by the scarlet of violence.

Men with faces seared and aged by the sun, under the same hats and clothes that their fathers might have worn and their fathers before them, tugged and pulled and dragged their cattle into the dusty traditional market.

Sheep stood tied together by their necks like bundles of hay. Oxen got pushed and dragged and beaten until they jumped up the backs of pickup trucks, only to wait for their fellows to join them until the truck was fully packed.

I wandered through the crowd of cattle and spotted one or

two yaks amidst the more common animals, looking surprised by their companions and incongruous in the heat under their thick coats.

Beneath wooden scaffoldings sweaty traders stopped to eat chunks of the same animals they were buying and selling and to sip that Uyghur drink made from chipped blocks of ice, wrapped with blankets to keep cool.

It seemed the way it had been for centuries, except for us gawking at them in both fascination and disgust, snapping photos and getting in the way of men and beasts alike, constantly at risk of getting stomped on by one bovine or another.

In one corner, a young man wielding a butcher's knife cut a sheep's throat. Then he proceeded to dismantle the animal that he had just slaughtered. I watched him work, at once mesmerized and horrified.

Blood drained from the gash in its neck out into a steel basin the size of a high school cafeteria tray, but some of it got onto the ground as well, congealing in the dust and blackening it like chocolate. The sheep's eyes were lifeless now, dead round things like marbles that kids might play with, staring into nothing. It seemed almost ridiculous, almost inconceivable, that a moment ago, before the fatal slash of the knife, there was in them that indefinable spark that we call life—animation, you might say, or spirit.

The young man cut off one of the sheep's forelegs and gave it to a little boy standing behind him while he worked on the rest of the dead animal, slicing away its skin and fur. Another sheep, presumably next, was tied up behind the boy and jumping and squealing and kicking against the wooden post in panic, confronted in the starkest way with the fate that was about to befall it.

The boy began shoving the lifeless leg of its fellow in its face with the sort of cruelty in which children so naturally excel. The sheep, now crazed with fear, squealed and kicked and pulled and jumped and writhed with all its strength, but to no avail. The phrase "like sheep to the slaughter" seemed not to apply.

There was one last fight in this animal. It would make no difference, not against man and his ingenuity, his knife and his rope. Not against such an overwhelming adversary. But no matter. The fight was there to be fought, so the sheep fought it, in the face of certain defeat and death. One might call it courage or honor.

When the fall was all that remained, it mattered very much how one fell. It was as true for a sheep as it was for human beings. I watched until I could watch no more.

3

THE LOST CITY OF THE POET

I WAS GOING to need a crew for this.

The *Hou Han Shu* gets cryptic after placing Gan Ying in the western extremities of today's Xinjiang. After stating that he hiked over the Pamir Mountains, the book next places Gan Ying in Jibin, or Kabul, Afghanistan (Jibin is believed to be a transliteration of Kophen, a Greek name referring to the Kabul River). That was a long way southwest from Kashgar.

On today's map, an attempt to ascend the Pamirs — perilous even for the well-equipped mountaineer — would mean heading into Tajikistan. A straight-line charge toward Kabul would mean threading the needle through the Wakhan Corridor, the narrow stretch of wild and mountainous land that is the only part of Afghanistan contiguous with China. Other travelers had hiked through the Wakhan before, including (possibly) Marco Polo, Sir Francis Younghusband, and Lord Curzon, once the Viceroy of India. But the Afghan-Chinese border in the Wakhan in my time was closed so that only smugglers were known to use the route.

Both the suicidal march to Kabul and the equally suicidal ascent of the Pamir, furthermore, would bypass great Silk Road cities including Bukhara and Samarkand. Although the *Hou Han Shu* did not mention either of these cities as part of Gan Ying's itinerary, it struck me as at least reasonable that he likely traversed them.

Even so, one did not undertake the crossing from China into Kyrgyzstan alone. Neither did one do it by public transport—there was none. The road from Kashgar to Kyrgyzstan was long. Whether one headed in a northwesterly direction over the Torugart Pass or straight westward to Irkeshtam, the thing to do was to gather a team of like-minded travelers heading the same way. I could credit myself with being the brains of the operation. But I wasn't going to be enough. I was on a quest. But they could have their own reasons for wanting to go; it didn't matter.

I found my first recruit at Theo's hostel, coming out of the shower with a towel around his lean waist.

Nik was from Switzerland but had actually been born in Danbury, Connecticut. Now he lived in Britain. He had variously worked as a personal assistant to temperamental photographers and as the editor of a trade journal. At thirty-two, he had the handsome face and closely cropped hair of a Prussian army officer, the ethics of a liberal pacifist, the lithe and lean body of a runner, and the stubbles of a backpacker not so careful with his appearance. And indeed, being Swiss, he had spent time in the military and knew how to handle himself. Also stereotypically Swiss, he was an excellent climber of tall slopes.

In other words, he was going to be useful.

Ben and Katie were from England. They'd been working in Hong Kong for the previous three years and were now taking the long way home. Both were tall and lanky; Ben was rather more Mediterranean looking and Katie more Nordic. Ben had a beard and a thin scar running down his forehead, which I fancied could be a battle scar, suggesting danger and a pugilistic anger in his personality that just might come in handy.

Katie unfortunately didn't seem to bring any obviously sought-after quality to the task at hand. She looked like the sort who might appear on a BBC scripted show — British TV attractive, not too attractive. And she had that English-bourgeois way of mumbling things like "That was quite nice, eh?" while obviously not meaning it. If we were to encounter difficulties along the way, I couldn't imagine her being able to passive-aggressive our tormentors into surrender. But hey, you never know. Besides, she and Ben came as a package. So that was that. I caught them halfway through dinner. They agreed to go with us.

Finally, we needed a local who knew the road and had a set of wheels that he was willing to place at our service.

The Night Watchman was supposed to rest during the day so that he could be awake and alert at night. The rules forbade him from moonlighting, or in his case, daylighting. But, lucky for us, he was none too scrupulous. For an adequate sum, he could be persuaded to break the rules and join our crew.

First, though, we had to hide.

Like a group of undocumented migrants, and as though the Night Watchman were our snakehead, the rest of us dived face first into his car parked outside Kashgar's long-distance bus station and kept ourselves horizontal to avoid being seen by his boss and colleagues. It was as though we were sneaking across the border. Wait — that was what we were doing, less the part about doing so being actually illegal.

Finally, the Night Watchman came to the car and took his seat. "You ready?"

Yes, yes, we replied.

"Let's go."

The Chinese border station was a long way away through a bleak, barren, and barely inhabited landscape. But it felt as though it took less time than it really did, because nothing of note stood beyond Kashgar until Kyrgyzstan.

At the border station, we paid the Night Watchman and bid

him farewell. This was as far as he could go. We'd have to find someone else to play the part of the local.

And here it seemed as good a place as any to stop for breakfast. The lonely restaurant servicing the border post, still well inside Chinese territory, was Kyrgyz, as evident from the signs. The rest of my crew looked at the Cyrillic writings and hesitated.

"I got this," I said and led the way as we pushed through the pair of batwing doors as though it were an Old West saloon.

Inside, a dozen Kyrgyz men were chatting. But they fell silent in unison as we entered and looked up with curious and not altogether friendly stares. I could picture pistols holstered against their thighs and shiny blades tucked inside boots. Tension hung in the air like an ancient, ugly curtain. For the moment it looked like the four of us crazy foreigners against the dozen of them local stevedores. I didn't like our odds, even with soldier Nik and boxing Ben by my side. Beside me, both of them imperceptibly coiled like springs.

"*Dobro utro,*" I said loudly so that the whole room would hear and with an injection of sunshine. That's Russian for "good morning."

Nik leaned in and whispered in my ear. "Bro, you speak Russian?"

The faces of the Kyrgyz stevedores as well as the proprietor, a Kyrgyz matron in late-middle age who had just emerged from the kitchen, cracked into a common smile. "*Dobro utro!*" they cried in a hearty response. The tension faded away. They went back to their breakfasts, even as several still stole glances at us.

Gingerly, we sat down at a table. The babushka owner came over. I asked for a menu. She laughed and gently explained, as though to a child or an idiot, that of course there was no menu. As was true throughout much of Central Asia, this restaurant served a grand total of three items, and most everyone knew what they were. There was certainly no need to write them down.

One especially inquisitive stevedore leaned over to eavesdrop on our conversation. I turned to face him.

"*Chto eto*?" I pointed at his bowl and asked. "What is that?"

"*Attala*," he said, or as least that was what it sounded like. It was a milky soup in a bowl. To this day I don't know if I heard the name of the dish correctly.

"*Attala khorosho*?" I asked whether it was any good, whatever it was.

"*Da, da*," came the predictable response.

I returned to the babushka. "*Attala, pozhaluysta*."

She nodded, pleased. Then she looked around at my Swiss and British companions. "How about you lot?"

"I'll have what he's having," Nik said.

Katie frowned a very English frown of disgust. "Nothing for us, thanks."

The babushka returned a few minutes later with our *attala*, which turned out to taste like a greasy, deep-fried sort of yoghurt. Nik valiantly swallowed a mouthful and then concurred that it was not entirely edible. Nomads had different tastes.

*****

The actual border was another hundred and forty kilometers beyond the so-called border station. And that whole distance was uninhabited. The Chinese left empty as no man's land a stretch wider than Israel-Palestine. Too close to the frontier, from their point of view, although you could fit an entire country in there.

As noted, we needed a new team member to play the role of the local. A Uyghur man offered his services as well as his van. We got in and were instantly reminded of the Kashgar livestock market. The back of the van had had its seats removed. If we were anywhere else in the world, it would look like a vehicle specifically modified to aid in the commission of certain crimes. Out here, though, the correct and more obvious conclusion was that the van was used to transport livestock, and said livestock had clearly urinated in it at some point, or more likely frequently. The sour, fermented stink initially overwhelmed the senses until in time, like frogs in boiling water, we all got used to it.

Meanwhile the abandoned landscape passed us by. Red-veined hillocks interspersed with cross-sections of gray like marble cake, wrinkles of rock and dust in the earth's worn face without the least hint of vegetation, rolling on and on with no suggestion that they would ever stop, as though all the earth should consist of these arid hills. In this character the land again reminded me of Israel, that barrenness that begot religiosity, that turned man's mind toward God or to creating one. It made sense. Looking around, you half-expected to find the Ark of the Covenant somewhere out here, in an underground chamber no doubt, waiting for the fated archaeologist to discover it.

Katie let out a cry, spotting a fox burrowing beside the highway.

Where the sheep van stopped, as far as it could go, a Kyrgyz soldier greeted us, looking like you'd imagine a Kyrgyz soldier: He was stocky, built like a tree trunk. He had three gold teeth that showed when he grinned. His eyes were hidden behind dark shades. In his hands, he was clutching an AK-47.

Was he it? Was he going to be someone we'd have to get past? Someone we'd have to bribe with that fistful of dollars? He certainly didn't look like someone we'd want to challenge overtly. If he chose to make life difficult for us...

Without a word, he pointed us forward. It took us a minute to understand that we wouldn't have to do anything to get past him. But we had to walk the remainder of this no man's land.

We got out of the sheep van, threw on our backpacks, and began the march. Besides a military watchtower set atop a hill, where I assumed a sniper was napping, there was no sign of human habitation. The same barren hilltops accompanied us left and right, watching us puffing under the weight of our backpacks in absolute and bemused silence. But a new element, a river, ran muddy and impatient to our right, as though trying to escape all this dryness that enclosed it like a cage.

Over a kilometer down this empty road, we entered Kyrgyzstan proper. And—damn it—for the third time today, we had to recruit a new local member of our crew, as the Uyghur man could not cross the border with us. It was beginning to feel like a Beatles-looking-for-a-drummer situation.

The good thing was that we had applicants. The difficult part was working out which one to trust.

We were on the road to Osh, Kyrgyzstan's second city. Half a dozen Kyrgyz men with cars gathered around us. "Osh? Osh?" they asked.

"*Da*," I said and then began bargaining in Russian. They looked at me askance as soon as the Slavic words came out of my mouth.

The leader of the pack, a bespectacled man in a baseball cap and button-down shirt like an office worker, studied me curiously. "*Kak vas zovut?*" he asked. "What is your name?"

"Vasiliy," I answered. My Russian teacher in college took to calling me that as the closest equivalent to "William." Its actual equivalent was "Basil."

The lot of them laughed heartily but good-naturedly, as though I just told a killing joke in the best comedy club this side of Tian Shan.

"Vasiliy?" they asked. "Are you Russian?"

"Don't I look like a Russian?" I replied and thought then that perhaps Professor Irina Andreevna would have been proud of her student.

They laughed some more. Just as quickly, the men agreed among themselves that the office worker with the baseball cap would be the one to join us. He introduced himself as Alyosha, the Russian diminutive for Alexey.

We hardly went five hundred meters, however, before Alyosha cried out, "Vasiliy! We stop for tea, okay?"

Not sure whether he simply felt he needed some fortifying before the long road ahead, I assented but added that we should only stop for five minutes. We pulled up to a country house, one of the scores that dotted this border village, with emerald mountains in the distance and old beat-up Soviet tractors and trucks in the foreground. Alyosha said it was his father's house and invited us inside. We sat down on rugs around a table and observed the row of teapots on the shelf, the half-eaten watermelon, and the simple country furnishing that would not have seemed out of place a century ago, or maybe even earlier.

His mother brought out tea, bread, and a sort of fried meat that I never got to the bottom of. Alyosha sat down with the rest of the crew. He volunteered that he was thirty-seven. Then he asked us each our respective ages and where we were from. I did my best to translate for the group.

"Very nice of you to invite us in for tea," Nik said.

"It is Kyrgyz hospitality," Alyosha replied.

Then he said something about his sister that I didn't understand until a few minutes later when we went back to his van. His sister, along with her three young children, including a nursing infant, would join us at least part of the way. She must have been waiting for her brother to drive her, but he wouldn't go until he found some crazy foreigners who would hand over cash for the privilege. The tea was surely Kyrgyz hospitality, but it was also a delaying tactic so that she could get ready.

We stopped again an hour later, this time in the village of Sary Tash. Here and throughout the drive, dramatic mountains ringed every stretch and every turn. On the sides of the road, horses and sheep roamed. Scattered around were occasional yurts, and men and women in traditional clothes appeared out of them now and then. It all seemed an image of the idyllic steppes. But for the power lines, one could very easily suspect that a quirk in the space-time continuum had sent one back to the age of Genghis Khan. In fact, the Kyrgyz countryside was perhaps more than anywhere else I had seen a place where this kind of time travel of the imagination was not only possible but easy, almost unavoidable. Sary Tash itself was little more than a collection of a few dozen houses, some roofless like broken Lego structures.

Alyosha announced that he had work, and a friend of his would take over the driving. He was apologetic, but that didn't stop us from feeling vaguely cheated by the switcheroo. For Pete's sake, the band's fourth drummer in one day?

The friend showed up a quarter of an hour later, a taciturn older man in a dark beret, driving a station wagon. I had assumed that Alyosha's sister and her children were stopping in Sary Tash. But then they got into the station wagon as well, the back-carriage area with the luggage, her three children on her lap. Remarkably, none of the children made a peep until they got dropped off a couple of hours farther along the way. Nomad parenting, I thought. They must have known something we didn't about kids.

At some point in the middle of the afternoon, I noticed our new drummer turning both palms upward and steering for a minute with his wrists while muttering something. Then I realized: of course, he was praying. Five prayers a day for the

Muslim, one in the middle of the afternoon, even as we sped along a bumpy road. Islam taught that one could pray anywhere, for prayer would make any patch of land holy through the act of worship. Even, I supposed, the rapidly receding asphalt under us.

*****

In college I developed a strange obsession with Kyrgyzstan. One day I decided that I had to go there. It had something to do with my coming across the forgotten episode of the Battle of Talas Valley. I very nearly wrote my graduation thesis on that event.

In 751 A.D., Islamic forces crossed the Amu Darya or Oxus River that today divided Afghanistan from Uzbekistan. Until that time, the nations on one side of the river had converted to Islam, but on the other side they had not.

The nations in the area asked China for help fending off these armed proselytizers of the new religion. It made sense: Tang Dynasty China was the greatest power in Asia. The Xuanzong Emperor sent an expeditionary force led by a Korean general, which met the Muslims at Talas Valley in today's Kyrgyzstan for a dramatic showdown.

The battle ended in disaster for the Chinese, if not necessarily for the world at large. Some of the prisoners of war taken by the Arabs were former paper factory workers. Their capture meant that paper technology, which had been invented in China centuries earlier shortly after Gan Ying's departure, escaped Chinese monopoly for the first time. And the Islamic world would eventually pass the knowledge onto Europe, making possible Gutenberg and the Renaissance, without which there would be no Western modernity, no Enlightenment, none of the great European empires, and certainly no United States. Back

72

in China, the distant defeat touched off a political crisis and the rebellion of 755, which nearly destroyed the Tang Empire. It was a pivotal event in world history but now largely forgotten.

Kyrgyzstan was also the source of a superior equine breed that the Chinese were desperate to acquire. The horses indigenous to China, today called Przewalski's horse, were short and stocky, embarrassingly outclassed by the nomads' steeds on a field of battle, so much so that the acquisition of superior horse breeds grew to be both a burning foreign policy concern as well as a psychological obsession. You can even see evidence of it in Chinese art: One of the most popular themes in Chinese paintings from antiquity until now is "The Eight Steeds." A common expression in the language most often repeated in zodiacal years of the horse says, "When the horse arrives, so does success."

Such was my preoccupation with Kyrgyzstan for a time that its very name, which I whispered tasting on my tongue the unvoiced "k" rolling into the voiced "g," its two "y"s like parts of a name out of science fiction, seemed redolent with the grass and sweaty horses of the steppes.

In my defense, at least my interests in Kyrgyzstan were based in actual history. Another person could just as easily have found such obsession in myths. Presumably surprisingly to most Western Judeo-Christians, Central Asian Kyrgyzstan, this land of Mongoloid and Turkic-speaking nomads whom most cannot find a map, claimed a deep connection to King Solomon of Israel.

Specifically, Osh, Kyrgyzstan's second city, was supposedly founded by Solomon. So said Kyrgyz tradition. I wondered whether a real-life Allan Quatermain ever came here looking for King Solomon's Mines. Indeed, a striking, stony quincunx dominated Osh's skyline, its silhouette dramatic against the setting sun. The locals called it Solomon's Throne.

I had my own quest to go on in this country. Not for the

mythical treasures of an ancient Israeli king, but for a very real place that was now nonetheless lost to history. As I couldn't expect my border-crossing crew to share the same enthusiasm for lost cities, I bade them farewell and headed northward to the Kyrgyz capital, Bishkek.

*****

Bishkek felt not like a city at all but an over-extended suburb with flat one-story houses placed tiresomely one after another, even as the snow-capped Ala-Too mountain range supplied a magnificent setting. Here and there aspirations were on display, if not necessarily Kyrgyz aspirations. Streets called Pushkin, Tolstoy, Gorky, Gogol, and Lermontov name-checked the heavy-hitters of Russian literature. Around the main square, the city made an effort at elevating itself above the level of suburbia. A bronze equestrian statue of Manas, hero of the Kyrgyz nation and of the longest epic poem ever written in any language at half a million lines, stood at the center of the square. But all around him, office buildings meant to be monumental in the brutalist Soviet style with their uncompromising angles and colossal arches looked rundown in their masonry blocks of faded, dirty white.

Before I launched my expedition into the Kyrgyz countryside, I had one logistical matter to take care of: my visa to Afghanistan.

I wasn't sure whether I'd even be able to get a visa. Few citizens of Western nations had recently tried. And reports of their experiences varied greatly depending on which Afghan embassy they approached. I had waited until I got to Kyrgyzstan, because the word on travelers' forums was that the Afghan embassy here was more pliable.

I found the Afghan embassy, a mansion with white-washed

walls, in a residential part of the city. One would have taken it for the home of a wealthy businessman, maybe someone in oil or mining, but for the bronze sign announcing "Embassy of the Islamic Republic of Afghanistan" and the lone security guard napping in a booth with reflective windows.

I knocked on the window. The guard came out. In my hesitant Russian, I explained that I wanted to apply for a visa. He told me to ring the doorbell. I did. A tinny voice told me to wait fifteen minutes. As I waited, two Kyrgyz men showed up and waited alongside me. The consular officer, a short and baby-faced man looking no older than myself, came out dressed like a student at the Sorbonne. The two Kyrgyz men made some complaint about petrol prices and then went away. The young officer turned to me. I said I wished to apply for a visa. He nodded matter-of-factly and asked what nationality I held. I said New Zealand. He asked to see my passport. I showed it to him. Then he gave me the application form to fill out and told me to pay the fee before returning the following afternoon to collect a thirty-day visa.

The next day I came back. The guard was watching a TV show on his phone. I buzzed the door again. A different officer, tall and gaunt, opened the door and invited me inside. I passed through the garden and ascended the stairs into what was a continuation of the theme of the wealthy businessman's house, a living room with well-appointed rugs. The key giveaway that this was a government building was a portrait of president Ashraf Ghani looking sternly down at whomever passed by from the wall.

The tall man showed me to an office to one side of the living room. A middle-aged consul, clearly the senior man, stood up from behind his desk to shake my hand. "*As-salaam aleikum,*" I said, giving the pan-Islamic greeting, peace be upon you. "*Wa aleikum as-salaama,*" he replied, and upon you be peace. He seemed to me a kindly, avuncular type. He had my passport in his hand, and when he flipped through it, I could see that it already contained a visa stamp. Another portrait of President Ghani hung on his wall.

"What is your name?" he asked. I gave my name. He nodded. "What is your nationality?" I said New Zealand. "But where were you originally from?"

"I was born in Taiwan," I said. "I think on the biographical page it states my birthplace as Taipei."

Again he nodded. "Where do you plan to visit in Afghanistan?"

"Mazar-i Sharif, Kabul, Bamiyan if I have time, and Herat…"

"Bamiyan?" He seemed mildly concerned about this.

"Well, if I can."

"Do you plan to fly from Mazar to Kabul or to go by land?"

"I haven't booked anything yet, but maybe flying is better?" I suggested, anticipating what he might say.

"Yes, you should fly. This is for your own safety. There is fighting with the Taliban on the road from Mazar-i Sharif to Kabul."

"All right, I will plan to fly."

"So I give you thirty days, starting today…"

Starting today! I had a few more days in Kyrgyzstan, and I had yet to get to Uzbekistan, the intermediate stop before Afghanistan. I would have less time than I expected in Afghanistan. I wore an expression of difficulty.

"It's just that I'm going to Iran afterward," I said, "and I didn't plan to get there until September."

"You have your visa to Iran?" I said I did. He looked at it. "Yes, it says you can enter now if you like, any time until October."

There was little point in arguing. The stamp was already in my passport with the dates printed. I thanked him and shook his hand again before showing myself out, still a little knocked off kilter finding myself walking through the embassy of

Afghanistan. The guard, still watching his show on his phone, didn't bother looking up.

I opened my passport and looked at the Afghan visa stamp. It had pink and green candy stripe patterns over a map of the country in silhouette, like a child's middle school art project. At the bottom, in font that made me think of travel agencies' shingles, was printed the name of the "Second Secretary (Consul)."

*****

Aliaskar came to meet me.

Years ago, I had made the acquaintance of an enterprising young Kyrgyz named Bolushbek in Shanghai. Or Boka as friends called him. Now I mentioned to him that I was in Bishkek. He was away when I arrived, but he told his "brother" (really cousin) Aliaskar about me, and the next thing I knew I was sitting at dinner in a Japanese restaurant with him and his friends Ramil, Fahria, Aidai, Akzhibek, and Karatai (another cousin), all young professionals and all speaking impressive English. Some had studied at the American University of Central Asia. All courses there, they informed me, were now taught in English.

Aliaskar worked in micro-financing. He had the thick torso of a Mongol wrestler and a stentorian voice like a big bronze bell. He was plotting a trip with his girlfriend, the willowy Akzhibek, to Vietnam and Cambodia. Hearing that I had been to Southeast Asia, he kept asking me for tips. Ramil in his turn informed me that he was of Hui extraction, a Muslim minority in China.

Then Aliaskar's face turned serious. "Why did you want to come to Kyrgyzstan?" he asked. "I mean really?" To many Kyrgyz, their country seemed so remote that any foreign visitor must've had a very good reason to be there.

"Ah," I sat back in my chair as I noticed that every face at the table was now turned toward me curiously. "Because I want to find Suyab."

"Suyab?" Aliaskar frowned.

"It's a place here in Kyrgyzstan," I said. "Or at least it was."

Aliaskar surveyed the blank faces of his friends. "Do you know what he's talking about?"

Suyab was once a Chinese garrison town, when it was known to the soldiers as "Suiye Cheng," or "City of Broken Leaves." Such was still how Chinese history books referred to the place. The Persian etymology of "*suy ab*," though, actually meant "toward the water." In 701 A.D., when it still fell under the jurisdiction of the Tang Dynasty, China's greatest poet, Li Bai, was born there.

I explained this background. But the faces around the table remained blank.

But Aliaskar had at least heard of Li Bai. "He was like the Pushkin of China, wasn't he?" he asked.

"Yes," I said, "yes he was."

No, he wasn't. Aleksandr Sergeyevich Pushkin was to Russian as Shakespeare was to English, a singular towering figure who remade the entire language in his own image. Li Bai was nicknamed "the Immortal of Poetry" and often considered the greatest poet of the Chinese language who ever lived. But a few other poets rivaled him in both artistry and reputation. His friend Du Fu, for example, "the Sage of Poetry," or Wang Wei, "the Buddha of Poetry." Setting aside the Tang Dynasty writers, there were also later figures like Su Shi who would excel in the Song style as Li mastered the Tang poetic forms, or the poetess Li Qingzhao, the Sappho of the East. Each of these figures can claim G.O.A.T. status in some way.

Nonetheless, Li Bai's stature was undeniable, having written some of the most memorable lines in the language's three-thousand-year recorded history. Some of Li's contemporaries believed that he was literally a living god, specifically the avatar of the "Great White Star" or the planet Venus.

History records that Suyab-born Li never saw China until he was perhaps five years old, when his father, a Silk Road merchant, decided to move back to the land of his ancestors. Presumably also because of time spent abroad, he was a polyglot. Today we would call him an expatriate or a migrant. Or as I liked to call individuals like him, anachronistically similar to the likes of Salman Rushdie and V. S. Naipaul, a transnational writer.

One of the many tales of Li's life says that one day an ambassador arrived at the Celestial Court from the kingdom of Balhae. Balhae contained portions of present-day North Korea, Manchuria, and the Russian Far East, and it was a predecessor state of modern Korea. The ambassador brought with him a hostile communique. But not one Chinese courtier could read the document. And that was the point: the ambassador had specifically come to embarrass the Middle Kingdom by underscoring its ignorance of the outside world.

Seeing this situation, the Xuanzong Emperor sent for Li Bai the linguist. But he was not home. Of course not—being a high-functioning alcoholic, Li was passed out in a bar somewhere. The Emperor ordered imperial guards to scour the capital for any sign of him. When they finally found him, they carried him into the palace.

Li had yet to recover from the previous night's drinking. Xuanzong summoned the palace chef to brew a hangover cure for the poet. Worried that the soup was too hot, Xuanzong personally waited on Li Bai, an unheard-of display of imperial favor for the poet. Having properly woken up, Li read the Balhae communique. Then he delivered the court's response to the ambassador both orally and in writing, rescuing the Tang Empire's honor for an afternoon. The ambassador was so impressed that, upon returning home, he advised the king of Balhae not to challenge the might of the Tang Dynasty. The Celestial Court, he told his king, had an actual god on its staff.

I was still telling Aliaskar about Li's many exploits when suddenly Ramil cried out.

"Oh! Oh! I know!" Ramil said excitedly. All of his friends turned to stare at him. "I remember now," he continued. "Yes, Suyab. I've heard of this place. It's near Tokmok, I think?"

Aliaskar smiled. "There you have it."

Oh, thank goodness, I thought. At least someone knew what I was talking about. I had begun to wonder if I hadn't fantasized the whole thing.

*****

To find Suyab, I was going to need a guide.

Kostya didn't look very healthy. In fact, he was downright emaciated. In a big city, I would have taken him for a drug addict, an aficionado of either cocaine or meth. Out here in staid, provincial Bishkek, I wasn't so sure.

And Kostya (short for Konstantin) wasn't Kyrgyz at all. His mother was Russian and his father Georgian. Indeed, he looked entirely Caucasian, not the least bit Turkic.

"Georgia is very beautiful," he made sure to let me know. No word, though, about the relative attractiveness of Russia. He wore a black Emporio Armani t-shirt and drove a Japanese car with the steering wheel on the wrong side. From the rearview mirror hung a wooden cross with orange ribbons.

He took me to be from China, and I didn't correct him. So he proceeded to tell me that his sister lived in Guangzhou and that he had tried learning Mandarin in college. "But it is very difficult," he said with a long, incredulous sigh, marveling at the language's peculiar difficulties.

What I needed to do, though, was to get him onboard with my quest. And I had to do it in Russian.

"Suyab, you said?" he asked with a frown. "Where is that?"

"Near Tokmok, apparently," I replied.

"I have never heard of it."

"Well, it's been destroyed for hundreds of years, so you wouldn't have."

"I don't understand," he shook his head. "You want to go to a city that's been destroyed?"

"Yes, well, you see..." I started rambling, looking for workarounds whenever I came upon something I didn't know how to say in Russian. "There was a great Chinese writer," I said, "who was born there." Then I remembered Aliaskar's imperfect analogy. "He was China's Pushkin," I explained.

"Uh huh," Kostya nodded. "Now you want to find the great man's birthplace."

"Precisely."

"Which actually no longer exists."

"Right again."

"So what do you actually expect to find there?"

"I don't know," I had to admit. "Maybe nothing. Probably nothing."

He pondered the matter for a minute, hand on chin. "Okay," he said finally.

"Okay, you will go?"

"Okay, I will go." For whatever reason, whatever flaw in his makeup, whatever disadvantageous mutation in his DNA, Kostya sympathized with me and my strange purpose.

But first, we made a stop at the Burana Tower, which was also near Tokmok. It and the surrounding archeological digs were all that remained of Balasagun, another lost city. A younger city than

Suyab, founded by the Sogdians in the 9th century, Balasagun overtook Suyab only to die as well after the Mongol conquest. Many Nestorian Christians lived here, after their version of Christianity fell out of favor in the West. The tower itself was actually a minaret built in the 11th century. A field of bal-bals, or petroglyphs, mysterious egg-shaped stones with faces carved into them like matryoshka dolls, lay to one side.

We pushed on to look for Suyab, which, unlike Burana, was not considered an attraction. Again and again we stopped to ask local farmers for direction, and half the time they threw up their hands, having never heard of the place. But Kostya persisted with remarkably good humor. Sure, it was a wild goose chase through the middle of nowhere. But he seemed to enjoy it almost as much as I did.

Following what directions we got, we drove down increasingly stony and bumpy roads until we came upon a pond in the middle of the trail. Kostya stopped the car as he eyed the pond gingerly. He got out, picked up a rock, and threw it into the water to determine its depth before turning around to say that his car could not pass. We needed a four-wheel-drive for this, which we had not had the foresight to bring.

"You want to try walking?" I said and got out. He looked at me with a plaintive expression. "Fair enough," I added to save him from his embarrassment. "You stay. I'll go on foot."

I began walking, splashing my feet in the mud around the pond. Behind me, Kostya looked on, seeming partly concerned and partly lost.

But just a few minutes later, a tractor with three farmers on it drove by.

"Suyab?" I asked. They looked at me nonplussed. Kostya caught up to explain far better than I could what we were looking for.

And, for once, these men nodded with understanding. For once, they seemed to have heard of Suyab. They proceeded to set us straight. I'd been walking in the wrong direction.

I got back in the car, and we drove where they pointed us.

Finally, amidst a field of tall yellow grass, we found an archeological dig, a pit in the ground, unmarked and unprotected, with nary an archaeologist in sight. Fifty meters farther — and I would not have recognized it but for its proximity to the dig — the undulation of the earth revealed itself to be the remains of ancient Chinese fortifications. The geometric regularity, which the layers of earth laid upon it could not fully disguise, made clear the nature of the structure. These were the walls of ancient Suyab.

I climbed up the wall, and Kostya followed after. I jumped off the wall and began wading through the tall grass.

"Be careful," he burst into English to make sure I understood. "Snakes."

That was enough to deter me from wandering in the tall grass any farther.

This was Suyab now, a handful of clues of the vibrant city that once was surrounded by long stretches of grasslands, ringed by distant mountains, visited only by farmers on tractors and quixotic me and poor Kostya whom I'd dragged along.

Underneath the grass and dirt lay Christian churches, Zoroastrian ossuaries, bal-bals like the ones in Burana, and the homes of a deeply mixed population of Chinese and Sogdians and Turkic peoples. And of course, the birthplace of China's greatest poet, without whom his country's culture would be much poorer. I liked to think that the multiculturalism of his upbringing held the key to understanding his art.

I glanced at the pit that the archaeologists left in the ground. Where did they go? When were they coming back? When would they finish the job? Digs took time, as I knew. But I sure would like to see their finds sooner than later.

I surveyed the empty fields around me, imagining 1,300 years ago the Chinese soldiers and the Sogdian caravans and Nestorian Christians cast out from Europe but happily worshiping God their way here and the Turkic horsemen passing peaceably by, ancestors of the Kyrgyz and the Uyghurs. The mountains beyond would probably have provided much the same natural background. But here, on the site of the lost city, all the fruits of human industry had fallen irretrievably away.

Kostya came over and stood beside me. I tried to explain to him further then why I wanted to see this field of nothingness. "In the year 700 or so," I told him, "the Chinese army was here and built these walls. And all of these different people and different cultures lived here side by side. Then a great writer was born here…"

My thoughts exceeded my grasp of Russian. But he nodded with understanding of what I failed to convey, with empathy for the vanished city I was trying to conjure. He put one hand on my arm as though to say that I didn't need to explain anymore.

Of course all of that was buried now. A thick blanket of earth covered the city, keeping it nice and snug as it slept its undisturbed sleep. It was a city that lived only in our memories, like the empire that built it. We left the dead where they lay, as one ultimately must do with the dead. Indiana Jones couldn't take the Holy Grail with him. So I, too, had to content myself simply with the memory of having stood here and having found the city's remnant.

*****

I didn't mind the slowness of the train to Issyk Kul, the pristine lake shaped like the country's lung. Once it was also a center of the Chagatai Khanate of the Mongol Empire. At least I didn't mind initially. I thought I'd enjoy the leisurely and scenic ride. Pulling out of Bishkek, the train, looking like a prop out of *Dr. Zhivago*, was mostly empty. I took a compartment of my own. But I should've known that the train would fill up along the way. An hour and half into the ride, a family of six descended on me, asking whether they could sit in my compartment. I said yes, not yet aware of what was in store.

The family consisted of an older couple, Arif and Evgenia, their daughter Karina, their son-in-law Bakha, and two young boys John and Azeri (at least these were the names that they told me). Mother and daughter both had hips as wide as the tractors I saw driving around Suyab. Bakha was Kyrgyz, and the rest of the adults were of that swarthier subset of Russian stock with dark hair and shadows in their visages and looking a little Iranian. But the two boys looked like such pure Aryan specimens that they could've been on a poster for the Third Reich. It seemed impossible that dark Asian Bakha was their biological father.

They asked me my name.

"Vasiliy," I said.

They got a good laugh out of that one. "Kiss my ass!" Bakha barked in English in response, laughing. I looked at him quizzically. Turned out it was the only English phrase he knew, and he would keep repeating it without regard for context for the remaining three hours of the ride.

Meanwhile the family brought out a fresh bottle of vodka. They began drinking shots, although this was 8:30 in the morning. By the time we arrived around 11:40, the bottle was almost completely empty.

I say the family, but Bakha did most of the drinking. Now he poured a glass for me and demanded loudly that I down the drink. "Kiss my ass!"

The family also brought potato salad in Chinese-made Tupperware (identified by the incongruous writing on the outside) and large chunks of roasted chicken. Now they offered me the food. "Eat, eat." This was Russian hospitality, the breaking of bread with strangers on a long journey and the forcible consumption of hard liquor, which I had experienced once before on the Trans-Mongolian Railway.

Then Bakha felt the need to go over once again their relationships to each other, pointing to Karina and emphasizing that she was his wife and the mother of the boys. I nodded. This genealogical explanation he would provide repeatedly, in between cries of "kiss my ass." He addressed me using the familiar form of address, "*ty*," while the rest of the family used the polite form, "*vy*," as one was supposed to with strangers.

Arif asked me my age. I said thirty-three. He said that this was a significant age in Russian culture, being the age at which Jesus died. I thought, don't I know it.

Bakha asked me my religion. Before I could answer Evgenia helpfully chimed in to announce that all Chinese were Buddhists. I went with this theory, as in many parts of the world it was hazardous to one's health to admit to atheism. Bakha said he was a Muslim then immediately violated the tenets of his religion by taking another shot of vodka.

Then, unprompted, he removed his shirt, revealing powerful shoulders and arms but an incipient beer belly. He reached out to squeeze my bicep, testing it before laughing dismissively, which made me feel I got a little less value for my money from my gym membership back in New York. "Kiss my ass."

He said he was twenty-seven and a boxer. I thought he looked older than I. I asked, with sarcasm that he missed, whether he was the champ.

"No," he said, shaking his head sadly. "Not even close."

I appreciated the honesty.

"You know Jackie Chan?" he followed up. What was it with people and Jackie Chan?

"I prefer Bruce Lee," I said.

Bakha began raising his fist and punching the air to show me his skills. "Kiss my ass." He said he had a match this coming Monday. The shirt never went back on until the train reached Issyk Kul.

Meanwhile the family gradually encroached into my personal space. One adjustment of the luggage here, one sidling up with the buttocks there. The two young and improbably blond boys screamed and cried and threw chicken bones at each other and spilled drinks all over the place. Karina hit them, and not only symbolically, which only led them to cry harder and scream louder.

Bakha pointed to Karina again and repeated to me that she was his wife. Then he made an obscene gesture conveying the sexual act. She slapped him on the shoulder. He told me she was pregnant. I sincerely hoped he was mistaken about that. "Kiss my ass." Giving up on sleep, I took out my book to try to read. This Bakha couldn't allow either. But with the bottle of vodka steadily emptying, his words even in Russian made less and less sense, until he was communicating mostly through grunts, punches thrown against the air, and the periodic ejaculation of "kiss my ass."

He began adding a middle finger to this expression, this *basso ostinato* in the fugue-like composition that he was making with his words and gestures. He looked at my book and mumbled something about not being able to read. Then he grew contemplative, which in him struck one as a scary sight. "Sorry," he began saying almost as much as he said "kiss my ass." Then he shook my hand with his own, stained as it was with vodka and chicken grease. "I like you," he said. "Sorry. Kiss my ass."

So it was to the accompaniment of the screams of children, "sorry," "kiss my ass," and under the generally bewildering siege that the family laid against me that I arrived at Issyk Kul.

There was no denying the lake's beauty, though. When the sun began to set over Issyk Kul on a fine afternoon, the shards of light scattered golden across the surface eddies like the definition of serenity.

*****

On my last night in Kyrgyzstan I finally caught up with Boka. He said I hadn't changed much, and I thought I could say the same thing about him. Maybe we had both gained some weight. But he was still the somewhat slight and unassuming young man that I remembered, not hulky like his cousin, Aliaskar.

We went to a restaurant that was a mock-up of a traditional Kyrgyz village with yurts, for horse meat noodles and sheep intestine and a drink made from wheat called *shoro* that had the look and consistency of chocolate milk but tasted more like sour cream.

"Until two generations ago," he said by way of explanation for the food, "we were still nomads."

He began telling me the story of his great-grandfather. "He was a very rich man—of course back then wealth was measured by the number of sheep you had."

"How many sheep did he have?" I asked.

"Don't know. But they said that when he took his sheep out on a mountain to graze, the mountain turned white. They went from mountain to mountain. And when they went to the river to drink, the river dried up. He had so many sheep, he used to trade them to the Uyghurs for watermelons: five sheep for five watermelons."

"That seems like a very bad deal," I observed.

"Of course it was, and watermelons to the Uyghurs were like dessert, not a meal. But he had so many sheep he didn't care."

Sadly the story didn't end well for the great-grandfather. "Then Lenin came, and Stalin. And they sent him to Siberia, to the gulag, because he was rich." Before he had to go, though, the old man buried his treasure somewhere. "It was — like Bambi..."

"Bambi?" I asked, confused. "What do you mean?"

"Like the cartoon, Bambi. A deer. A golden deer."

"Like a statuette?"

"Yes, a statuette, made of gold, of a deer. He buried it in the mountains. The clues were that it was under this tree by this rock, and so on. We never were able to find it again."

"That's too bad," I said. "Should've given better clues." Boka shrugged.

But Boka wasn't one to wallow in sad memories of a lost golden deer. He was already on his fourth start-up, an education agency sending young Kyrgyz students to study abroad. He owned a honey farm in the countryside. And he was starting an event-organizing company to bring educational agencies in different countries together. He spoke of men like Steve Jobs and Elon Musk with fanboy enthusiasm, which led him to speak of America with equal enthusiasm and admiration.

I asked him whether he was familiar with *The Great Gatsby* and said my bit about how it lay claim to being the Great American Novel, because of this hope against hope in Jay Gatsby that was so quintessentially American, that made him the "great."

Boka nodded but then pointed out that Daisy was married to Tom and that Gatsby's whole enterprise was to get a married woman to leave her husband and be with him instead.

"In Kyrgyz culture, he would be totally in the wrong. Tom could totally shoot him. Okay, maybe Tom's not a good guy. But it doesn't matter. You can't go around trying to get another man's wife."

He was right. And he had a wife of his own now, so I supposed that he knew what he was talking about. But he only highlighted the way that the best of American optimism was also always some sort of transgression.

The conversation turned to my travel plans. I explained to him my concept of replicating Gan Ying's mission to Rome. "You know I like history," I said.

Noting that I was heading to Afghanistan, we got onto some of the most gruesome episodes of the Great Game. There was the tragedy of Alexander Burnes, a uniquely gifted explorer, diplomat, and bestselling writer, hacked to pieces by a Kabul mob.

Then there was the disastrous British retreat from Afghanistan in 1842, following a completely unnecessary war, when all 16,000 or so Britons and Indians died on the road from Kabul save one Dr. William Brydon who hobbled into British India, like Ishmael alone to tell the tale. Brydon would later inspire Arthur Conan Doyle in his creation of Dr. John Watson, a British army surgeon wounded and traumatized in the Afghan war who returns to London to find solace in friendship with a great detective.

"They actually trusted them," Boka shook his head in disbelief, meaning the British trusting the Afghans promising that they would let them go peaceably. "I would never trust these people if they promised me safety."

But he seemed to enjoy the idea of following in an explorer's footsteps. "My favorite Chinese explorer," he said, "is Zheng He," bringing up the eunuch admiral who sailed multiple missions in the early 15th century. Chinese tradition says that the castrated Mongol Muslim representative of the Ming court reached at least East Africa. With his honorific title, "San Bao," Zheng might have been the inspiration for Sinbad in the *Arabian Nights*.

*****

For now, my adventure in Kyrgyzstan was at an end. I had found what I came to find, saw what I came to see. And there was necessarily a kind of melancholy in a quest completed.

Regardless, it was time to ride into the proverbial sunset.

4

LAST YEAR IN SAMARKAND

"THEY'RE SO weird over there," Boka had said plaintively to me over dinner, referring to Uzbekistan. He was not wrong.

We may as well begin with the matter of money. How much exactly was the Uzbek currency, the som, actually worth? The Uzbek government insisted that 2,580 soms bought you one U.S. dollar. Economic forces put the figure closer to 4,500. But you could only get anything close to that rate on the black market, by making private and illegal exchanges. Any transaction done through a bank or with a credit card had to be priced at the fictional, state-imposed rate.

And as the largest som bill was only 5,000 or slightly more than one U.S. dollar, black market exchanges involved bundles of bills thick as bricks. Impossible to fit into wallets and almost impossible to count, these must be carried around in paper or plastic bags as though meant for drug deals. A great many Uzbeks sought to take advantage of newly arrived foreigners through this unusual state of affairs, including the first person I met in Uzbekistan, greasy, shifty-eyed Igor.

What kind of government would maintain a fictional value of its own currency? The kind comfortable with fictionalizing a great deal more, of course. A few months earlier, President Islam Karimov had "won" "reelection" with over ninety percent of the "votes," in an "election" in which ninety-one percent of "voters" "turned out." The Uzbek government stuck to this narrative as firmly as they stood by the nominal value of the som.

Then there was the fundamental issue of the alphabet. Which one was it? When Uzbekistan was a part of the Soviet Union, the Uzbek language adopted the Cyrillic alphabet of Russian, with some adaptations. In the years since the dissolution of the USSR, the Latin alphabet gradually began to take over. But the shift was far from complete. Many shop or street signs were still in Cyrillic. And often the two alphabets got mixed up with each other. One grocery store proudly proclaimed itself a "MAPKET": the Cyrillic "r," derived from the Greek "rho," looked essentially the same as a Latin "p," obviously causing the confusion. That's not to mention a pre-Soviet period when Latin letters were used and the even earlier practice of using the Arabic alphabet.

The palpable Chinese influence in this country also added to a feeling of strangeness. Indeed, all the flotsam and jetsam of Chinese industry here came with an overwhelming sense of incomprehension. Machines and material objects everywhere bore the Chinese language logos of their manufacturers, from trucks to tractors to forklifts or even refrigerators in convenience stores and trash cans in lobbies and beer glasses on the table. None of those meant anything to the local Uzbeks. An oversized digital clock hung above the doors of a mosque, bizarrely informing the congregants what date it was on the Chinese lunar calendar. In a children's playground, a candy-colored rocket ship had the Chinese characters for "China Aerospace" painted on the side.

Tashkent, Uzbekistan's capital, expressed the basic surrealism of life in Uzbekistan through its architecture, if only inadvertently. In Bishkek, I had complained of its feeling of suburbia. Not Tashkent, which favored colossal buildings and public sculptures and broad avenues and oversized traffic circles. The ordinary citizens of Tashkent went about their lives and their everyday concerns in their intimidating shadows.

At the heart of the city, Karimov at the time of independence from the USSR in 1993 built a park and a statue dedicated to Timur the Lame or Tamerlane, the conqueror and empire-builder whom Uzbeks considered their national hero. The iconography was not big on subtlety: Karimov cast himself as another Timur, never mind that the former Soviet apparatchik had not accomplished a small fraction of what Timur did.

I walked through the park and sat down on a bench obliquely across from the equestrian statue, the horse with its left foot raised, the rider with his right hand outstretched in a gesture meant to herald some brilliant future. Farther along, shops lined the avenue, and Uzbek families were out for their evening strolls. But whatever their domestic happiness, they were enjoying it in the context of the inhumane city that enveloped them and the corrupt and authoritarian government that ruled over them. It was like watching a family actively trying to ignore a burglar rifling through their belongings even as they sat at dinner.

Directly across the square was my hotel. The Hotel Uzbekistan, a honeycomb of windows bent into a horseshoe shape around the traffic circle, was one of those ugly concrete Soviet monstrosities designed for the small numbers of foreigners allowed in back in the day. And back then (or who knows, maybe even now), the KGB must have bugged every room.

I surveyed this monumentalism around me. And the more I chewed on it, the more it took on a nasty taste, this celebration of dictators, authoritarianism expressed through architecture and city planning. It was architecture as propaganda.

I realized with surprise that I now missed Bishkek's uninteresting suburban look, its sense of being simply a collection of houses in which people lived and got up in the morning to go to work and came back in the evening to be with their families and to go to sleep. There was the simple liberty of citizenship in it in a way that Tashkent with its massive structures and grand parks could not evoke. There was a quiet dignity in ordinary people going about their lives that self-aggrandizing monuments could not produce, because in the end they celebrated only the corrupt, the megalomaniacal, and the empty.

On the park bench, I couldn't help but exclaim—if only silently and to myself: "They're so weird over here."

*****

I made a quick dash across the country to Nukus. The dash meant that I got a rapid survey of half of Uzbekistan. As a country, which is to say, as a land, it stood in sharp contrast to the green hillocks of its Kyrgyz cousin. The words "lunar" and "Martian" are far too overused in the descriptions of arid landscapes, but much of the country did bring to mind the surface of one of earth's less populated planetary siblings, pockmarked with impact craters. Presumably that also went some way toward explaining the impression the Uzbeks gave off of being somehow warped—too many desiccated days in the sun can do that to you—and the feeling that events did not occur here according to any general logic.

Nukus, Karakalpakstan, didn't really exist as more than a small settlement until 1932, when the Red Army built its chemical weapons research institute here, precisely because of its isolation. If Nukus got wiped off the face of the earth, few would have even noticed.

In fact, the town had that Los Alamos, makeshift "military secret in the desert" kind of feel. Walking around its chessboard streets, I began picturing pale Russian scientists ambling down the nondescript streets, clutching clipboards, squinting in the unfamiliar sunlight, absentmindedly mumbling something to themselves about endothermic reactions. Actually, Los Alamos might be too mild a comparison. Nukus felt like Area 51. Or some post-apocalyptic town in an episode of "The Twilight Zone."

And if you were thinking that "Nukus" and "Karakalpakstan" sounded like made-up names, well, other towns in the area included Moynaq and Hojeli. All the names sounded like the inventions of sci-fi writers, their rings no less fictional than names like Cthulhu or Klendathu or Klingon. As I wandered around Nukus, I couldn't shake a persistent suspicion that I was actually on the 1950s set of a B-movie production, a sci-fi or horror picture about aliens from outer space or monsters born of a military experiment gone wrong. At any moment, I thought, the director might step out from behind the soundstage, script in hand, breaking the fourth wall as he yelled, "Cut!"

The region of Karakalpakstan also contained the southern half of the Aral Sea, or rather its etiolated corpse, one of the most bizarre and nonsensical sights on earth.

It didn't begin that way. The Arab scholar Ibn Rusta first referred to this body of water as the Aral in 903 A.D. "Aral" meant "island." The ancient nomads who came upon this body of water in the middle of a harsh Eurasian landmass considered it an island of life in an ocean of desolation. At the time it was the fourth largest lake in the world, behind only the Caspian Sea to its west, Lake Superior in North America, and Lake Victoria in Africa. But in the space of just over half a century, man in his infinite absurdity had almost completely destroyed it.

Beginning in 1960 or so, for the sake of growing cotton, the Soviets diverted the two rivers that fed the Aral, the Syr Darya and the Amu Darya. The Aral had been shrinking ever since, a trend unabated when Uzbekistan gained independence and

Karimov continued the old Soviet water policies. Kazakhstan to its north did nothing to help.

From one big lake the Aral transformed into two smaller lakes, to four even smaller lakes, to one much diminished strip of water retreating to the west. And most of the former lakebed was now a new and polluted, diseased desert of salt plains and chemical waste from industrial dumping and pesticides to the fallout from Soviet weapons tests. Instead of an island in a sea of desolation, now it was emphatically a part of that desolation.

I went out to the township of Moynaq, formerly a center of the Soviet fishing industry on the southern coast of the Aral. Now the lake had retreated to over two hundred kilometers away, leaving the town high and (literally) dry.

Formerly on an isthmus connecting a peninsula to the shore, the town was once accessible only by a bridge. The bridge now stood over a pathetic little pond like one that anyone with a big house might have in the backyard, a tiny remnant of the former reach of the Aral. It was as though the townspeople engineered for the little water that remained to gather under the bridge just so that the embarrassment of the bridge's utter pointlessness wouldn't be absolutely complete.

The town itself was barely populated now. Coming down its one long main street, I passed by empty house after empty house, from which sun-scorched ghosts might emerge under white sheets, too thirsty to spook anyone, begging for a drink of water. On either side of the main street hung propaganda posters featuring beaming soldiers in uniforms and smiling teachers and grandparents hugging grandchildren, adding to the effect of absurdity. But the merciless sun had bleached almost all the colors out of their smiles.

Halfway through town, I spotted a massive billboard of an ophthalmologist or optometrist, showing a woman's eyes, just

97

the eyes, blown up and staring down at all who dared to pass by. It was as though a deliberate staging of Dr. T. J. Eckleburg's billboard from *The Great Gatsby*, looming over the valley of ashes between Long Island and New York City. Only there, Dr. Eckleburg's billboard watched over the American industrialism of the 1920s, a tragedy in the making. Here the Uzbek doctor's billboard bore witness to the aftereffects of Soviet industrialism of the 1960s, a tragedy already made, as well as the continued indifference or ineffectiveness of the Soviets' successors. And Moynaq was a kind of valley of ashes, or more literally a port of dust. And then there was the irony of an eye doctor advertising here when, due to the environmental catastrophe, the local population suffered all manners of illnesses from drug-resistant tuberculosis to anemia to various forms of cancer. But okay, doc, let's make sure to get them some glasses so they can see better their families dying before their eyes.

At its height, Moynaq had a fleet of some five hundred fishing vessels. Now one boat stood at the center of town, next to the municipal building, as a kind of memorial. A former cannery to the north of town had been torn down. A statue of a fisherman, beaming at the heavy fish he just caught and now held in his hands, formerly stood at the town center. But it had now been relocated to the dark and musty town museum. Perhaps its mockery was too much to bear. A startled museum custodian came and turned on the lights when I showed up. I was the only visitor in a space that felt like a mausoleum.

Another ten or so ships lay beyond the northern quay, or what was once the quay, where the Aral once began. A flight of stairs took me down from the former shore to the former sea. The ships lay on the lakebed, dried up so long now that brushes had sprouted out of the sand. But broken shells and layers of salt covered the sand here and there, testifying to the recent emergence of this desert from a sea. Storms of salt and sand blew out from it like some biblical curse misplaced in time — the Aralkum or "Aral sand" blew ninety days out of each year, spreading toxic chemicals all around. I could just about picture Lot's wife here, turned into a pillar of salt for having looked upon the destruction of Sodom.

I walked among the ships, peering through the punctures in their hulls. Completely rusted over now and the color of tea leaves, the empty husks of the ships lay silent like dead insects with their insides hollowed out and their little legs sticking up in the air. They were contraptions made by man, for the benefit of man, and now they were made useless by the folly of man. Graffiti messages showed on this hull or that. One of them, written in chalk and in English, read: "SAVE THE SEAS." A poignant message at the center of desolation.

Beyond this graveyard of ships, the former Aral Sea stretched far into the horizon. Beyond that were oil refineries breathing fire and smoke in unabated exploitation of the corpse of the Aral. The Ahabs of greed would not stop until they cut away every piece of the great dead whale's blubber, until they made use of and therefore made useless every bit of the lifeless body. Oh horrible vulturism of man, from which not the mightiest ocean is free.

Somewhere over the horizon was also Vozrozhdeniya ("Rebirth") Island, formerly home to a Soviet biological weapons facility. Science fiction returned to my mind, the dystopian futures of poisoned landscapes conjured by writers' imaginations or cinematographers' lenses, here made reality, here made visceral, here made now. One could easily believe that some horribly disfigured creature, the result of a Soviet science experiment, lived amidst radioactive waste on the ironically named Rebirth Island, or in a deserted underground bunker, howling into the concrete darkness.

I thought of Gan Ying and what message he might have been bringing with him. Confucian philosophy also taught that man ought to dominate nature, to triumph over it. One could sympathize with the ancient origins of that thought—the annual destructive flooding of the Yellow River and thus the need to control it. One of the earliest, semi-mythical kings of China was the hydraulic engineer who "tamed" the river and in so doing won political support. But that was the same sort of ideology that, extrapolated to its extreme conclusion, would lead to this bone-dry shell of a sea that now lay spread out before me. It was the ideology that Gan Ying would have carried with him in his soul as the ambassador of his civilization. It was what he would have spread, whether intentionally or inadvertently.

For the first time I felt a bit glad that he failed in his mission. But then again, the Chinese were hardly unique in their struggle with nature. Did those Anglo-Scotch-Irish-German settlers of the American Frontier not seek at every turn to enlarge their dominion over nature?

I asked Pulat, a twenty-six-year-old father of two daughters, what was there to do about the Aral. "Nothing," he shrugged. "It's finished."

*****

With that thought of despair, I returned to Nukus.

Incongruously and adding to the sense of the surreal, this dusty and now toxic, waterless backwater of the former Soviet empire also hosted one of its the best art collections. Both the *New York Times* and Newsweek had run features on the Savitsky Museum, a fact that it proudly trumpeted through clippings in a glass cabinet. But it was so short on visitors when I arrived that its staff turned on the lights on specific floors as I, solitary as an

Emersonian in the woods of Massachusetts, ascended the stairs and approached them.

It shouldn't have been left so lonely. Igor Savitsky had come out here as part of Soviet archeological missions surveying the ruins of Central Asia, and he wound up both settling in this most unlikely of places and rescuing a whole collection of art. Deemed too contrarian in the urban centers of the Soviet Union such as Moscow and Leningrad, these works found toleration here in the forsaken Nukus.

It was hard to see now what was so controversial about most of these pieces. To my eyes, they were as uncontroversial as the plaster copies of ancient Greek and Egyptian sculptures also found here. Some of the paintings and sculptures were avant garde or fauvist. But right next to them were more traditional works that seemed a throwback to the likes of Cézanne. One painting by a man named Sokolov looked like another take on Monet's "Impression, Sunrise." Savitsky's own none-too-original work was in this vein: sun-bleached landscapes of the Central Asia around him and the ruined castles therein, dominated by bright hues of yellow and pink. These pictures reminded me of a couple of other Monet paintings of beaches and rocks in the sea and a handful of images by J. M. W. Turner. A blown-up photo of Savitsky loomed over one corner of his museum, looking sensitive and effete, a Stellan Skarsgard type.

Another corner of the museum was dedicated to the Aral Sea. In the Perestroika era, under Gorbachev, the Soviets could finally acknowledge the epic environmental vandalism for which their country was responsible, including the death throes of the Aral. Posters from the late-1980s hung on the walls, calling for the government to save the Sea.

Even then, the fishing industry here was already dead. One image of the lakebed pierced with a pipeline and bleeding black oil stuck with me. Obviously the call went unheeded. Or perhaps, with the entire Soviet empire on the verge of collapse, Kremlin politicians simply had more immediate concerns, or at least concerns more directly related to their self-preservation. These colorful calls of Cassandra now kept appropriate company with the banned art from an earlier time.

*****

I left Karakalpakstan behind and headed southeast toward the old Silk Road towns, one town at a time getting back on the faded trail from nineteen centuries ago.

Halfway to the old slave market of Khiva, and a fortress stood shaped like a wedding cake left out in the oven of the sun. This was Chilpyk-Qala, one of the old forts of the khanate of Khorezm or Khwarezm.

Khorezm was not exactly a country Western kids nowadays learn about growing up. But it played pivotal roles in forgotten moments of world history. It was a perceived insult from the king of Khorezm that served as Genghis Khan's pretext for launching his westward campaign. Without it, and the Mongol Empire might not have stretched all the way to Europe.

And one of Khorezm's favorite sons, Muhammad ibn Musa al-Khwarizmi, invented algebra in the 9th century. And "al-Khwarizmi," meaning "of Khorezm," transliterated into Latin, gave rise to the word "algorithm." All the tech bros in Silicon Valley would have nothing to talk about today if it weren't for him.

Khiva was, from the mid-16th century onward, Khorezm's capital. Just as the people of Osh claimed King Solomon as their founder, so local Khivan tradition claimed that Shem, son of Noah, founded this city. Shem was additionally supposed to have dug a well here that he called "Kheyvak," from which the current name of the city derived. That same well that the son of Noah dug, again so they claimed, one could still visit. That exact well, from soon after the deluge receded, if you can believe it.

The firmer evidentiary footing of archaeology showed that the city existed by the eighth century A.D. but not necessarily in Gan Ying's time. If it already stood here, then the oasis of Khorezm must have seemed to the Chinese ambassador wondrous after so long in the desert, like shore after many weeks at sea.

Khiva was a trading post on this branch of the Silk Road. The Mongols rode in, in the 13th century, and conquered Khorezm like they conquered everyone else. But then the Mongol Empire fragmented, and Khorezm broke free from its successor regimes, the White Horde and the Chagatai Khanate. The Khorezmi rebuilt their capital in the city of Gurganj or Urganch. But then Timur, the next great conqueror of the steppes, destroyed Urganch in 1388. The center of life in Khorezm moved to Khiva, which became the capital under the Uzbek Shaybanids in 1592, as the empire of Timur came to its own demise. Khiva then attained a dubious distinction as the great slave market of Central Asia, selling kidnapped souls including Slavs. Indeed, the English word "slave" comes from "Slav."

The Russian expedition of 1717 didn't much help their Slavic brethren. Led by Prince Aleksandr Bekovich, the expedition ended in a slaughter of the Russians similar to the slaughter of the British in Afghanistan over a century later. Nadir Shah of Persia followed after the Russians in 1740 and succeeded where Bekovich had failed and made Khorezm an extension of the Persian empire. The Slavs would finally have their revenge in 1873, when General Konstantin von Kaufman conquered Khiva in the name of the Czar.

*****

"We've met," Marco said.

"We have?" I asked with a frown.

"In Tashkent. We stayed in the same hotel."

"We did?" I tried to remember him, tried to picture his dark Mediterranean hair and whitening stubbles in the hotel lobby. He was dressed in the boots and dusty khakis and shirt of an Indiana Jones type, less the hat and whip but with the sweat-stained knapsack. I had no memory of him. "I'm sorry to say, but I don't recall meeting."

"That's okay," Marco shrugged.

"What's your name again?"

"Marco," he said with an exaggerated roll of the "r." "This here is Monique," his companion for this trip.

Marco and Monique were both middle-aged Italians from Milan, and both worked in the art world. Monique was into textiles and the decorative arts. Marco was a scholar of the old Italian masters from Leonardo to Caravaggio and represented Christie's, the auction house, in Italy. To him, all things Italian were superior to all things not. In his career he had traveled the world looking for exiled works of these masters turning up in unexpected corners like Tashkent. A kind of treasure hunter for dislocated paintings.

"Stalin," he explained to me, "decided that every town in the Soviet Union needed a museum, to educate the people. But these provincial towns didn't have any art to show, so he had the museums in Moscow and St. Petersburg send their pieces over to the small towns. The result is that you can find works of Old Masters in random places all over the former Soviet Union."

Still, I could dredge up no memory of our initial meeting. Was I supposed to have met Monique then as well?

Regardless of my inability to recall them, Marco and I took a long walk together around the entire length of Khiva's old crenellated walls.

Mud and straw were the preferred building materials in this desiccated part of the world, unlike with fortresses in damp Europe. But somehow the walled city reminded me of Dubrovnik, the republic by the sea in today's Croatia. I said as much to Marco, and he agreed but insisted on calling Dubrovnik by its old Venetian name, Ragusa.

The atmosphere of the once proudly independent khanate was most pronounced atop its romantic city walls. They snaked around an encirclement that was impressive pre-industrialization but that now seemed small in our Malthusian age. And yet suddenly our age receded, and we had the sense of stepping back in time to an era that was more brutal and brutish but perhaps also more brilliant in its triumphs as well as failings. Birds perched atop battlements fluttered into the sapphire sky as I came too close, picture-perfect against the sun.

As we neared the end of our walk, the sun began to dip over the western and main gate, and Khiva was bathed in the warm glow of the golden hour like bread dipped in honey. It was remarkably and almost improbably beautiful. It was the sense of nostalgia and wonderful loss you feel when you wake up from a dream of a pure and happy summer's afternoon long ago, in an age of childish innocence.

We made our way to the Kalta Minor, the third and only unfinished major minaret that overlooked the city. It was one more symbol of ambitious folly — as though the world needed more of them. The local grandee, Mohammed Amin Khan, began building the minaret in 1851. He proclaimed that by the time it was finished, it would be tall enough for a man standing on top of it to see the rival city Bukhara, hundreds of miles away.

But the Khan dropped dead four years later, and construction stopped, and no one ever found out whether it was really possible to see Bukhara from atop the tower. Its broad base covered in tile patterns of turquoise and beige and green and yellow, though, definitely spoke of a certain Babel-esque ambition and grandiosity.

As the sun set over the Kalta Minor, which stood near the western gate of the old city walls, there was a transcendent beauty in it, a loving ambiguity in the way the expiring sun reflected off the tiles, a coquettish charm in this inevitable withdrawing into silhouette and the darkness of night.

*****

So many of the historic buildings of Khiva were once madrasas that one wondered whether the town was really a university in disguise.

The madrasas all had the same basic layout: a vestibule entrance with corridors leading to one hall on each side, followed by a courtyard at the center of the building surrounded by a series of monastic-looking cells for the students to study in.

A few of the buildings that were not designed as madrasas, however, proved the most rewarding. The Juma Mosque, the present incarnation dating from the eighteenth century, contained a forest of wooden pillars. A few of these pillars, lovingly carved as they all were, were remnants of the original mosque from the tenth century. Later in the afternoon, when the light that seeped through the central atrium began to fade and the mosque darkened, the forest of pillars took on a ghostly appearance and reminded me of the underground, Roman-built Basilica Cistern in Istanbul. Some of the old capitals were Sassanian in design, foreshadowing what I was to see in Iran.

Similarly haunting was an old palace, now used as a museum of handicrafts. Its stately courtyard rivaled Alhambra in Andalusia, and blue tiles patterned the space like a magical cuirass on some demigod. Blue as the color of heaven directly above our heads.

And the mausoleum of Pahlavon Mahmud, patron saint of Khiva and wrestling (as a legendary wrestler who supposedly defeated an Indian opponent to secure the freedom of Khorezm), attracted me both for its beautiful tomb chambers and the imam sitting ready to dispense religious teachings to the faithful.

Pahlavon was a Sufi, a member of that mystical sect of Islam that emphasized the inward search for divine truth. Ten years earlier I had read *The Conference of the Birds* by his fellow Sufi and Persian poet Farid ud-Din Attar. "It was in China, late one moonless night," the poem begins, "that the holy bird Simorgh "first appeared to mortal sight." Because as the Prophet Mohammed once told his followers in a hadith, "Seek knowledge; even as far as China."

China to Attar, and even to Mohammed and his companions, was the symbol of an experience so distant that it might as well have been mystical. China meant the end of the earth, as Rome meant to Gan Ying and his peers. In the poem, the Simorgh calls upon a company of thirty birds to make an arduous pilgrimage across alien lands to the Simorgh's home atop the mountain of Qaf. After many hardships, the thirty birds arrive at their destination but find no avian god. Only then are they reminded that in Farsi, "*si morgh*" means "thirty birds": Through the transformative journey, they have become the god whom they sought.

*****

Then, unbidden, the air of the bizarre and the grotesque returned to haunt me. But of course, unbidden is always how the strange and the uncanny return to us.

The Khivans now used the interiors of many of their historical buildings as museums. I made a circuit through them, curious of what I might find but not expecting too much. In the art museum, a handful of paintings by local artists filled just two rooms, one dedicated to realistic pieces (some looking like the artist had been to school in France) and the other reserved for Dali-esque fantasies but all involving Central Asian elements.

In the entirely uncalled-for natural history museum, stuffed muskrats shared space with stuffed chickens, and the next room such quotidian objects as apples and watermelons. All the stuffed animals were consonant with the fur hats they were selling outside, which seemed unseasonably warm to me and entirely inappropriate to this climate. And yet Uzbeks actually wore fur on their heads even in August. The room after the apples and watermelons held snakes in jars, but somehow the formaldehyde never came up high enough to cover the entire snakes, so that the copperhead's brows lurked above the fluid, menacing like the head of an alligator.

The formaldehyde didn't stop there. And the strangeness I first experienced staring into the dead eyes of the copperhead was about to rise to another level.

In one of three history museums, none terribly informative or with much to show, a double-headed dead baby lay preserved in a Tupperware box. The seams were all taped up, but it looked like an amateur job. The label said the specimen was from 1970. Four eyes closed, one mouth open, the conjoined twins were of a putrid lime color, a sight out of horror flicks. All the descriptions were in Uzbek, but I gathered that the exhibit was supposed to show something about fertility and childbirth in the area. Whatever its reason of being, unique and jarring next to old pamphlets about family planning, the dead baby was an incongruous and revolting freak show.

Across from the dead baby was a portrait of Sayid Islam Khoja, one of Khiva's former viziers, looking every bit the dashing young hero. It was a name that seemed to me nothing but titles: "Sayid" denoted supposed descent from the Prophet, "Islam" was of course the religion, and "Khoja" indicated lordship in Persian and the Turkic languages. Sayid was an early 20th century modernizing liberal, and for his efforts the khan and the imams murdered him. So perhaps, it occurred to me later, the dead baby with two heads made a fitting commentary on the vizier's stillborn career.

*****

As luck would have it, the regional melon festival was taking place in Khiva. I had never been to an American county fair, but I imagined that this and that might have shared a great many commonalities. Pyramids of sweet melons and watermelons piled up beneath stages and platforms set up for the occasion. Young women and rather older men in costumes danced on the platforms. Women quick with knives cut slices of melon and shared them among all who attended, and later children and adults alike made off on their heads with the same melons that made up the pyramids, as many as they could carry, a cornucopia.

A bigwig in a black suit pushed through the crowd, or rather his goons did before him like a snowplow. Behind him followed a train of older men wearing the traditional embroidered hats (just like the ones I saw on Uyghur heads in Kashgar). Some women in costumes were dancing in the middle of the festival, inviting the few foreigners to join them. But the arrival of the bigwig interrupted them as his people cleared a path. A different group of men, slightly younger, in freshly pressed white short-sleeved shirts, awaited behind the dancers to shake hands with the VIP, and beside them were three police officers in blue fatigues.

On the stage, two pairs of MCs were speaking. A pair of women on stage left, and a man and a woman on stage right. The man wore a red bowtie and a red pocket square that together rather screamed. His partner in a maroon traditional dress translated what he said into English. Now and then, feedback in the mic pierced all our ears. The bigwig arrived between the two pairs and gave a speech at the lectern. It was all in Uzbek so I didn't understand a word, but clearly it was as boring to those who could understand as it was to me.

I asked someone who the bigwig was. "Mayor of Boston," he said. Boston? But he was referring to the nearby town whose name happened to be spelled the same as the one in Massachusetts.

And even as he spoke the bustle of the melon festival didn't stop for one minute. Young men and women in kaleidoscopic costumes began dancing on the platform of the Kalta Minor. Marco joined me to watch. One young woman, not in costume but in black t-shirt and jeans, joined in. She danced with some skill but not professional competence, but there was charm in the amateurish abandon with which she threw herself into it.

"That girl is very beautiful," Marco said with longing.

*****

Marco and I shared an enthusiasm for Robert Byron's classic travelogue, *The Road to Oxiana*, which recounts Byron's journey in the 1930s from Venice across the Middle East to Afghanistan and finally India. "It's why we're all here," Marco said admiringly, "because we read his book!"

But, in discussing Byron, I explained my travel plans, noting that I'd have to go through Afghanistan for my project. Marco grew grave upon hearing it. Nearly simultaneous bombings had just taken place at a Kabul police academy and near a U.S. military base. He told me a story about a trip to Yemen some years ago.

"I hired this driver," he said, "who wore a sword at his waist. We drove out into the country. In the middle of nowhere, up a hill, this jeep came up to us, and all the men in the jeep got out. They all had Kalashnikovs, and they came toward us, saying something in Arabic that I couldn't understand. I tried to smile and be friendly and said I was Italian and a tourist. One of the men, the leader, kept coming toward me, and at five paces away he loaded his Kalashnikov. I thought, 'Well, what can you do.' Then he handed me the gun. I didn't know whether to take it. But he insisted. So I took the gun. Then he told me to fire it. So I did. Then all the other men loaded their guns and fired into the air. Turned out that was how these tribesmen welcomed strangers. But who could've known?"

Upshot, he told me to fly low and move fast. Undoubtedly good advice.

*****

The desert of Kizilkum, meaning "red sands," lay between Khiva and Bukhara. Traversing the desert now and then I caught sight in the distance of Amu Darya, and along its banks stretches of pasture. The pale blue slick of the water, with the oily verdure surrounding it, was a sight surprising to the point of miraculous amidst the red sands. As we rounded a corner in the desert road, a tiny tornado blew up a pillar of dust like some biblical apparition. Far away the aluminum roof of a farmhouse reflected the sunlight in my eyes, blinding like a diamond.

The driver, a stocky man named Azim who talked too loudly

when he got on the phone, abruptly stopped the car, got out, and slipped a bill inside a little red wooden box by the roadside. I asked him what that was for. He said it was baksheesh for the cemetery, pointing at a scattering of gravestones a little farther from the road. Presumably he intended to enjoy the protection of the dead.

As we approached Bukhara, a column of black smoke rose like an ancient smoke signal. When we got closer, I saw that the mouths that breathed out the tongues of fire and trailing clouds of soot were oil pipelines. The weird and dystopian ghosts of the Aral had pursued me here as though looking to avenge some wrong I didn't know I'd done them. A part of me wanted to scream out of the window: "It wasn't me! Stop following me!"

Azim said the pipelines were new and built by the Chinese. Indeed, one highway sign as we passed was written in Chinese and Russian. They were the new Greeks — beware of them bearing gifts.

What gifts might Gan Ying have brought with him? By the time he set out from China, Bukhara was already seven hundred years old. Its population, though, was likely very different from what I saw. Turkic peoples didn't migrate into this area until the sixth century A.D., and later incorporation into the Persian empire brought Iranians. But in the city's Ark or citadel I came across a tantalizing hint at the history of interactions with China as far back as the time of Gan Ying.

The Ark was the oldest extant structure in the city, dating back to the fifth century. But the Red Army under General Mikhail Frunze leveled a good part of it in 1920. The exterior walls, though, largely survived Soviet bombardment. The walls had a gentle way of tapering parabolically upward, wider at the bottom. And the mud bricks made rounded corners, not sharp radiating angles like in European designs but voluptuous curves that gave the building the aspect of a whale or, yes, an ark. Wooden beams protruded through the walls, exposed liked studs on a Chinese aristocrat's door, holding up the walls and adding to the appearance of a biblical ark meant to rescue animals two by two.

Inside, the surviving rooms housed exhibitions on the history of Bukhara, drawing on sources including the *Hou Han Shu*. According to the Uzbek display, Chinese chroniclers referred to Bukhara as "Buhe," "Buho," "Ansi," or simply "An." I had my doubts about the transliterations here and in particular the monosyllabic "An," which, representing only one Chinese character, was unlikely to be the proper name for a foreign nation. But "Anxi" was the Chinese transliteration in the *Hou Han Shu* of "Arsacid," the Parthian dynasty that ruled Persia from 247 B.C. to 224 A.D. (Although confusingly, "Anxi," with one different character and tone but the same Romanized spelling, also meant "To Pacify the West," and it was the name of the prefecture that the Han Dynasty set up in Kuche. Put another way, Gan Ying's journey likely took him from Anxi to Anxi—from "To Pacify the West" to the land of the Arsacids.)

Bukhara was part of Sogdiana, which never unified as a state but remained a province of Persia. The Sogdians might have been Iranians or the Scythians that Herodotus mentioned. Much of the population in ancient Suyab back in Kyrgyzstan was Sogdian. And the rebellion that racked China in 755 was led by a man, An Lushan, who was likely Sogdian. (There's that character again, "An." Perhaps he took it as his surname to indicate his ethnic origin. And his given name, Lushan, would have been "Roshan" in Persian, meaning "brightness" or "light.") An immigrant not quite accepted by his adopted country, the most powerful country in the world, turned around and tried to destroy it. There was a lesson in there somewhere.

Across from the Ark and designed as a junior version of it stood the *zindon* or dungeon. Two British officers, Lieutenant Colonel Charles Stoddart and Captain Arthur Conolly, were imprisoned here, mostly in the infamous *kanakhona* or bug pit, a twenty-two-foot-deep hole infested with scorpions and rats and other assorted vermin.

Stoddart arrived in 1839, as Britain was invading neighboring Afghanistan in the First Anglo-Afghan War. His mission was to reassure the emir, Nasrullah Khan, of Britain's intentions. But, rudely in the emir's eyes, Stoddart brought no gifts. And the letter he did bring was from the governor-general of India instead of Queen Victoria, Nasrullah's sovereign equal. The emir sent him to the *zindon*.

Two years later, Captain Conolly came to negotiate Stoddart's release. But he ended up the colonel's cellmate when the emir decided that Conolly was part of a British conspiracy.

After Britain's ignominious retreat from Afghanistan, the emir had both men beheaded. Friends and families of the two officers raised money to send yet another emissary, this time a German clergyman who had converted from Judaism named Joseph Wolff. Known as "the Eccentric Missionary," Wolff showed up in Bukhara wearing full canonical garb. According to Wolff's own memoirs, the emir laughed hysterically upon seeing his appearance. The sight of a white man wandering around Central Asia in the cassock and purple sash of a Lutheran clergyman was simply too bizarre and incongruous. For the amusement provided and for that reason alone, the emir declined to execute Wolff but let him live to tell the tale.

All this cruelty and buffoonery in the name of the lightheartedly named "Great Game" — a phrase Conolly himself coined and Kipling popularized. Did Stoddart and Conolly play a game of chess against black-robed Death in the bug pit? Or did

Wolff on a deserted road to Bukhara?

*****

They called Bukhara "the Pillar of Islam," and it was supposed to be the holiest city in Central Asia. Its many mosques and madrasas would attest to this reputation. Timur's grandson, Ulugbek, built the oldest madrasa in Central Asia here in 1417. Many other madrasas have since copied its design.

Clothed serenely in its blue tiles, the Ulugbek madrasa had a gentle dignity to it, as though conscious of how original it was and how imitated it would become, how little it had to prove. The Abdul Aziz Khan madrasa, directly opposite the Ulugbek but built over two centuries later, had to try hard to rival its predecessor. A wondrously colorful facade of gold and blue and orange and pink painted in floral designs and carved like beehives announced the building's unabashed ambition.

Another madrasa that went for flash and bang was the Nadir Divanbegi. They had built it as a caravanserai. But then the khan mistook it as for a madrasa, so then the architects had no choice but to convert it into one. Its exterior, in blatant violation of the Islamic prohibition against depicting living creatures, showed two phoenixes or peacocks, or the holy Simorghs of Attar's poetry, flanking a sun with a human face in it, like an image of Ahura Mazda, the Zoroastrian god. The phoenixes in turn clutched a pair of lambs in their claws.

Another spot of blasphemy, or multiculturalism, as we would see it now, was the twelfth-century Maghok-i Attar mosque. It was built on top of a Zoroastrian temple from the fifth century, which in turn was built on top of a ruined Buddhist temple. And until the sixteenth century, the Jews of Bukhara used the mosque as a synagogue at night. On its wall hung faded photos of visits by Madeleine Albright and Hillary Clinton. The Jewish school was a block away. To the south of the old city lay the Jewish cemetery. Except there were hardly any Bukharan Jews left: they'd mostly packed up for Israel.

How much more interesting would this city be if Buddhists and Zoroastrians and Nestorians and Jews still lived alongside the Muslims and each other as neighbors? I thought of Philip Roth's proposition in *Operation Shylock* that Jewish culture flourished only in the diaspora. But perhaps the thought said more about me than about Bukhara, that I would contemplate permanent exile as preferable to having a home and being among one's own. Most people get homesick after too long away from where they grew up; I get anxious after a while being surrounded by people who look like me.

More orthodox was the Kalon Mosque with its gorgeous turquoise domes and the sapphire and baby blue tiles occasionally dipping into green and a reddish brown. There were no depictions of living things here, only geometric patterns of alternating six-pointed stars and hexagons, and the names of "Allah" and "Mohammed" in Arabic enclosed within them. Compared to the sacrilegious phoenixes and lambs and sun with a human face, the effect was less gorgeous but more sublime. The same patterns on the facade as well as in the interior created a thematic unity that felt at once delicate and sincere.

Just outside the mosque, the 1127 Kalon Minaret shot up proudly into the sapphire sky. Genghis Khan was said to have been touched by its beauty when he sacked Bukhara. He ordered it spared while his men burned the rest of the city. Frunze's army damaged it but failed to bring it down. It was indeed a remarkable work of architecture. Fourteen distinct ornamental bands encircled it, some geometric patterns and some Arabic inscriptions, all beautiful with that contemplative serenity that was quintessential to the best of Islamic art.

Farther east and much younger was Chor Minor, a Tajik name meaning "four minarets." The building was an 1807 entrance vestibule to a vanished madrasa. Technically not minarets, the four towers above it huddled together to give an impression of stumpiness. But with the towers' turquoise domes and the vestibule between them like a brick and mortar yurt, the entire structure had the beauty of an intricate jewel box, containing within it some unimaginable treasure. What could it be? Enlightenment? But now the interior was taken up with a vendor of trinkets much less precious than the box that contained them.

*****

Outside the old city's hammam or bathhouse an elderly man with a bald head, wizened beard, and very tanned skin was playing chess with a younger man whose slightly European look betrayed the complicated genealogies in this part of the world. The younger man had duties to attend to in the hammam and offered me his seat. Was it strange that not long ago I had pictured Colonel Stoddart playing chess against Death?

I sat down and opened with the Queen's Gambit.

Despite his white beard, the old man played with a teenager's rashness. His hat, a black and white classic Turkic design that I saw in the bazaar of Kashgar, lay to his side next to the porcelain bowl of tea that he would from time to time refill. He had let drop one slipper and folded his right leg in front of him. Now and then he would scratch the rough and dry skin of his bare foot, a fairly revolting gesture. When he made a move he often grumbled. When I made a move that put him in a tough spot he would say, "okay, okay," not to indicate acceptance but defiance. When he saw something, he would indicate it all too clearly by tapping the piece in question. When he put me in check he would say "shakh!" with youthful vehemence. (The English word "check," in the context of chess, comes from the Persian "shah," i.e., king.) And when each game ended, instead of shaking the hand I offered him he slapped it away dramatically.

I thought I had him as our first game approached denouement, but then the younger man, clearly the superior player, returned from his duties and pointed out an error on my part. Then the old man demanded a rematch, which allowed me to redeem myself. With one game each, I thought it was a gentlemanly time to plead a prior engagement.

*****

Within earshot of our little chess game, shopkeepers bargained with tourists in fluent French and Italian. The occasional "konichiwa" or "nihao" came my way. How easy it was now in our age of jet planes to travel. Or at least, to get to faraway places. Fitzroy Maclean, in his book *Eastern Approaches*, recounted how difficult it was even in the 1930s for him to travel through the Soviet Union to Bukhara, shadowed by NKVD spies. Never mind Gan Ying at the end of the first century, bobbing up and down the back of a camel, perhaps making his way by night to avoid the heat of day, under the dome of brilliant stars. Now anyone with a credit card to buy a plane ticket could come to Bukhara, a city once almost mythical. And this fact came with the inevitable commercialization. Uzbek merchants cried out in Italian — "signor," "prego," "grazie." And the Abdullakhan Madrasa was one big carpet shop now, albeit an atmospheric one.

What then distinguished travel, elevated it above mere tourism? A higher purpose, I had thought. But what made this higher purpose anything more than a conceit? When everything is known, what is left to discover?

Something within our souls, I suppose, where the Sufis also sought their truth. Because travel still holds its transformative quality. The crossing of borders and frontiers will change you, even imperceptibly, even without you realizing it. Because boundaries are where the most interesting things happen, where different peoples and cultures and ideas meet and spark. Because besides physical borders, the traveler crosses the great invisible boundaries of human life, racial, linguistic, religious, which are more important still.

My preoccupation with the notion of translation becomes in retrospect one with travel as well. Not for nothing does the Russian word for "to translate," *perevodit'*, literally mean "to drive across." And the condition of feeling like a translation of myself is really the condition of living on the *limen*, on the boundary between countries and communities and cultures.

The world issues its challenge: "I dare you to step across this line." And the traveler (and the translator) shrugs and says okay. This must have been why I was attracted to America in the first place, because America is the frontier, is made by the ever-shifting frontier. Even the Atlantic coast was once the frontier of Europe. The frontier can be a place of prejudice, for sure, a line that divides us from them, a construct that allows those within to proclaim those without to be savages. Like the Great Wall. But the frontier also attracts the dreamers and doers, the misfits and outcasts, Jack London and Mark Twain. And crossing the frontier transforms the traveler, as a book in translation is never quite the same as the original, as the pilgrimage transforms the thirty birds into the holy Simorgh.

*****

Samarkand was the political heart of the Timurid empire. As Tashkent demonstrated that architecture is always a political art, so the architecture of Samarkand left no doubt of its pride of place, dwarfing everything in pious Bukhara and gemlike Khiva. Indeed, it dwarfed the human person who must exist within its spaces.

The Bibi-Khanym Mosque was a prime example. A giant mass of masonry, its scale was so grand that it was impossible to relate to it on a human level, however wondrous the structure might be. Confronted with its enormous facade, I felt breathless both because of its beauty and the sense of stony oppression. The enormous weight and mass of it bore down on the individual human beings craning their necks like children looking up at a god. Indeed the blue tiles spelled "Allah-u-akbar" high above: "God is great."

The grandiosity that alienated the individual reminded me of Moscow, the so-called "Stalin wedding cakes," enormous buildings meant to humiliate the individual with his puniness. In fact, the Soviets were enthusiastic restorers of the Bibi-Khanym and other grand structures of Timur. Made sense. But the Bibi-Khanym had a saving grace: small decorative elements on the walls plated with silver and gold so that they shone delightfully like winking eyes, as though telling the visitor not to feel too intimidated after all.

But architecture was also a weapon against mortality, however inadequate it might be against the profound inevitability of death. Still, bricks and mortar, if assembled with sufficient vision and skill and care and taste, could outlive any human being by many years or even centuries. When Gilgamesh found the plant of immortality only to lose it again, he built the first human city, Ur, as recompense.

Perhaps Timur and his descendants built their wondrous

Samarkand for the same reason. These buildings that rose from the earth like giants, titans, in some way challenging God, even if the Muslims in these princes could never admit to such idolatry. But structures like Bibi-Khanym announced man's ingenuity, man's power, man's ambition, what man alone among all of earth's creatures could accomplish if he put his mind and his two hands to the task.

There was desperation in the protest, of course, this hope against hope that one's work would last, because obviously it wouldn't, not forever. So the structure inadvertently also announced man's frailty. And deep in his soul he knew that nothing that he did that didn't last could truly matter.

As for Timur, shortly after his artisans finished laying the silver and gold on this grandest of mosques, he died while initiating yet another military campaign, this time against distant China. The Hongwu Emperor, founder of the Ming Dynasty and my ancestor's liege, true to tradition, had treated Timur like a vassal. So Timur decided to teach the man a lesson. But then he died. Pneumonia, not even a soldier's death, in the winter of 1405. So Timur's buildings far outlived him as well as his empire.

I paid the lame emir a visit in the mausoleum he shared with his sons and grandsons. The magnificence of the exterior reminded one that Timur was more than a bloodthirsty conqueror but also a great patron of the arts and the builder of these astonishing cities. But inside a map of Timur's campaigns greeted me, with so many arrows in so many different colors indicating his numerous marches against numerous adversaries that the map looked like an indecipherable PowerPoint presentation.

Above it hung a portrait of Timur, looking every bit the mean old man whom he at least eventually became, a man all too familiar with cruelty. A man who swept away entire countries with entire peoples in them. This was the man whom Uzbekistan had adopted as its national hero. But in the tomb chamber one grew sympathetic to Timur again. The cerulean and gold sarcophagi chamber with the fluted dome was of such beauty that against all logic I felt half convinced that the souls celebrated within had to have been equally beautiful. The angelic sight transfixed me.

And then, without warning, everyone started praying. They had their hands outstretched, palms open and facing the gorgeous dome, and they chanted their prayer, low and solemn, a spiritual murmur. It was as though the mausoleum had suddenly transformed into a monastery, and I was surrounded by monks, in a time to keep silent. It was a truly odd feeling to find myself suddenly standing in the middle of someone else's religious ritual, a ritual that I couldn't truly understand.

Everyone was praying but me and a Russian mother and daughter on the opposite side. Self-consciously I took off my hat and held it awkwardly in what I thought was a respectful gesture. The daughter, a pretty teenaged blonde, grinned at me or rather at my sheepishness.

*****

Here were Marco and Monique again, standing outside Samarkand's famed Registan. Did I agree to meet up with them? They said I did, as they said we'd met before. Had we become friends without me knowing it? Or were we still strangers who, like fallen leaves on the surface of a pond, happened to drift into one another?

We walked through the Registan together. It was another example of this architecture of intimidation, albeit again an incredibly beautiful one. The three madrasas that made up the complex might individually not give the impression of political power, but together as a triptych in a horseshoe formation with a massive square in the middle it seemed one of the great political theaters on earth.

The madrasa of Ulugbek, the oldest of the three, stood to the west. That remarkable man, Timur's grandson, was simultaneously a ruler and a great astronomer. The sunburst motifs atop the facade of his madrasa served as admiring commentary on its builder's study of the heavens. Inside, alongside predictably brilliant plaster carvings of *ghanch* work, an exhibit celebrated Ulugbek's scientific achievements: the crater on the moon named after him, the Latin translation of his tract on astronomy, the 1843 English compendium of his work (still circulating four centuries after he lived) alongside those of Ptolemy, Tycho Brahe, and Edmund Halley of the comet's fame.

The Tilla-Kari or "gold-covered" madrasa at the center seemed to continue this celebration of the great scientist emir, with its flowing golden curves like those intricate epicycles that medieval astronomers wrongly but charmingly drew to explain the movements of planets while assuming that the sun revolved around the earth.

Finally, on the east, stood the Sher Dor or "lion" madrasa. An orange pair of the titular lions, looking more like tigers, took up flanking positions on the facade. Before them ran white deer, the objects of their pursuit, and behind them a pair of human faces peered out through crowns of sunburst. Another blatant violation of Islamic stricture, it inspired in the viewer the excitement of transgression.

Taken together, the three madrasas looked like a sacrilegious humanist Islamic Holy Trinity. And the overall effect was that of utter grandeur. Of course visitors snapped photos endlessly, I among them. Beauty is that which inspires the desire to possess and the desire to replicate. This is why we take photographs of beautiful things, so that we may imagine that we possess them, however delusional that belief, and so that we replicate that beauty, even if only as a poor facsimile.

Afterward we paid a visit to Ulugbek's ruined observatory on the outskirts of town. There, through bone-chilling nights when the prince could have rested in comfort in his harem, Ulugbek made his measurements of the heavens, still the most accurate astronomical data available even into the nineteenth century.

Carl Sagan said it best about the Pale Blue Dot that was earth when looked back upon by the Voyager space probe: One speck of dust among many, suspended in light. All that every king and emperor and every prince and potentate had ever fought over was no more than a small fraction of a dot. Every race of foreigners with their religion supposedly anathema to ours come from a fraction of the same dot neighboring our own. Timur's empire was such a tiny fraction, but no doubt he considered himself a great man.

Perhaps Ulugbek understood better than his grandfather ever could the impermanence of human endeavors on earth. He must have understood it, having spent all his evenings gazing up at the heavens from his stony observatory, eschewing the pleasures of the palace to keep company with the sparkling stars of the seemingly eternal constellations. And, without his astronomy, we could never have sent Voyager into interstellar space, and it could never have turned its gaze back on the planet of its makers to show them what ingenious idiots they were: clever enough to discern distant worlds, foolish enough to kill each other over small portions of their own.

He should have stuck to science, and he probably preferred to do so, was more at home in his observatory than on the throne. But royal birth placed the responsibilities of government on the shoulders of a scientist. In the political intrigues and infightings among Timur's descendants, Ulugbek wound up beheaded by his own son and was later buried beside his grandfather Timur.

"Let's face it," Marco chimed in when I mentioned the manner of Ulugbek's death. "Haven't you wanted to do that to your own father? I know I have."

*****

Frustratingly for me, all of the grandeur of Samarkand that I saw postdated Gan Ying's mission by some fourteen centuries. Ancient Samarkand, known as Marakanda to the Greeks, was what Gan Ying would have seen. It was that city that so impressed Alexander the Great when he conquered what was at the time the capital of Sogdiana in 329 B.C. What Alexander said then still rang true today: "Everything I have heard about Marakanda is true, except that it is even more beautiful than I ever imagined." Except the visitor today was impressed by an entirely different Samarkand.

How astonishing to think that the brilliant city of the Timurids might have been but a poor replacement, an understudy, of the lost original. The original, a major capital by the time of Alexander's conquest and a Silk Road metropolis, survived the Arab conquest and the ensuing turmoil to grow into a larger city than its modern progeny. Then in 1220 Genghis Khan arrived to raze all that splendor to the ground. When a thousand desperate defenders of the city barricaded themselves in a mosque, Genghis set it aflame and condemned the whole lot to a fiery death.

Today the old Marakanda lay as an archeological site just outside the heart of modern Samarkand. A vast field of undulations lay under thick layers of dirt and clumps of yellow grass. Standing atop what underneath might have been part of someone's home or the public bath, I tried to imagine the vanished glory. And what desolation the survivors of the Mongol onslaught would have found, when all the killing and burning were done, standing atop some broken walls as I was doing, surveying their beloved golden city now lying in smoldering ashes.

A colossal, fascinating seventh-century mural dominated the center of the museum dedicated to ancient Marakanda, at one end of this field waiting to be dug up. The left-hand side panel showed the Sogdian King Varkhuman of Samarkand and his spouse. The central panel depicted ambassadors from China presenting gifts to King Varkhuman. These ambassadors came here six hundred years later than Gan Ying and were dressed in Tang Dynasty clothing instead of the Han fashion that Gan Ying would have sported. Still, the scene might not have looked much different when he passed through Marakanda and presented his diplomatic credentials from the emperor of China.

The panel on the right-hand side showed the Chinese emperor himself hunting with his retinue, a larger than life figure, depicted as young, handsome, and heroic. It fascinated me that the Samarkand artists would show the Chinese emperor opposite their own monarch and arguably upstaging him. The vigorous, heroic portrayal as well as the timing — early- to mid-seventh century — meant that the subject was probably Taizong of Tang, possibly the greatest monarch in Chinese history. Perhaps that explained the flattering portrayal: Taizong's reputation as the Khan of Khans so preceded him that in Sogdiana it was acceptable to give him precedence over the local king.

*****

I sat down in a local courtyard restaurant for lunch. I asked the waiter what they had. "Soup and shashlik," the answer came.

The already very limited Uzbek menu had diminished here from the usual five options to two. I ordered the shashlik, or kebab.

Out of nowhere a stranger spoke to me. He was sitting at the next table, a middle-aged man with salt-and-pepper hair and a tiny bit of stray coriander on his right cheekbone.

"Korea?" he asked. I had been asked one variation or another of the "where are you from" question enough times by now that I wished that I had a dime for each occasion. I told him I was Chinese, the complete answer too long and complicated and maybe even fantastical in many parts of the world.

"Ah, Chinese." He paused for a moment before following up further in Russian. "Are you here on business?"

"No," I said, "just traveling."

He waved his hand dismissively, almost spitting at my answer, as though it was a ludicrous proposition to travel for anything other than business. Then he recovered from the unwelcome information.

"Chinese, very smart," he said, pointing at his own skull with one finger. "When they come do business in Uzbekistan..." he allowed his sentence to drift off but made a throat-slitting gesture across his neck with his thumb, combined with a maniacal grin on his face. Then he straightened that thumb to indicate approval.

"Very smart," he repeated the throat-cutting gesture. "Chinese, very good." Point at brain, cut throat, thumbs up.

"Well," I said awkwardly. "Enjoy your lunch." I refocused my attention on my shashlik.

Right then he picked up his food and moved over to my table as though I had just invited him.

"China," he put out one hand with five fingers spread out, then with his other hand he measured out one finger at a time: "America, Germany, Britain, Italy, Russia...." The meaning seemed clear enough: he considered China a match equal to all those other countries combined. I wasn't so sure, but a nuanced discussion of international political economy was beyond my knowledge of Russian. "China," he said, thumbs up again. "Russia," thumbs down. "America," thumbs down again.

I pointed out that nine out of ten refrigerators I saw in shops, supermarkets, or hunched over by street vendors in Uzbekistan were not only Chinese made but of a specific Chinese brand. "What?" He seemed genuinely surprised.

I noted the name of the brand, Xing Xing or XingX.

"Oh, that's Chinese?" He asked. It seemed strange to me that he could have not noticed the ubiquitous presence, even monopoly, of one foreign company with its logo plastered all over the country. Then again, I could read the text on the fronts of those refrigerators, which he presumably couldn't.

He started talking about his own business and his experience with the Chinese and saying how, with his cooperation, a Chinese businessman — naturally intelligent in his view — would get terribly rich in Uzbekistan. Hint, hint.

He asked me what I did for work.

"Lawyer," I said. This was one of the downsides of telling people not the whole story of who I was; they all assumed that I lived and worked in China. My answer got him quite excited. Slowly and with several repetitions I tried to explain to him that I was not looking to participate in any Uzbek joint venture any time soon.

"How's the soup?" I asked, seeing that he had gone with the other option on the menu. He assured me that it was very good. Then he made a gesture with his hands to indicate an erection and laughed. What a terribly optimistic belief, I thought, that the commonplace Uzbek soup had the effects of Viagra.

"Shashlik too," he pointed at my food and made the gesture of massive erection again. And again, with such strange optimism that almost seemed heroic. The only two dishes this restaurant had available, and they both promoted the male libido? What were the odds? "When I was a young man, when I was eighteen," he made another obscene gesture, this one with both hands and a thrust of the hips under the table.

I could do nothing but laugh politely. "You're a very funny man," I said.

"How old are you?" He asked me, again a very common question.

"Thirty-three," I said.

"How many children do you have?"

"I don't have any children."

"Thirty-three and no children!" He smacked his forehead as though he had just heard the most absurd tragedy. "I have five children!" After a moment's pause he made the point that one wanted to be around still to see one's children grow up. No doubt this was true, but the local life expectancy necessarily figured into this particular calculus. "That's life," he said. "Wife, children; that's life."

"I don't even have a wife," I said.

"You're not even married?" Again he looked at me with the utmost incredulity.

"It's not that unusual where I come from," I said. He looked at me skeptically, weighing my mendacity.

"You should eat shashlik every day," he said, "and the soup." Then again, the fist and the raising of the forearm to indicate a comically enormous erection, followed by a pounding gesture. "And have children." Then he paused.

He said his name was Arik, fifty years old, and not Uzbek but Tajik. I heard in fact that a large proportion of the Samarkand population was Tajik but wrongly recorded as Uzbek. The waiter came over and told me in English how much I owed. I paid him.

Arik pointed at the both of us and asked how it was possible that we could talk to each other.

"He's speaking English," I informed Arik. Marveling at this discovery, he walked me out with one arm around my shoulder and shaking my hand profusely as though we were old friends.

*****

My final stop in Uzbekistan was Termez. The name of the town was supposed to have derived from the Greek word "thermos," because when Alexander the Great passed through here, the hot climate here made a deep impression upon his Greeks. But it was comfortable enough when I arrived, once I got past the Uzbek soldiers at checkpoints with AKs painstakingly writing down every detail in my passport. It was a border area, so they were extra vigilant.

"But you're Chinese, right?" the soldier said looking over my New Zealand passport.

"Well, as it says here, I was born in Taiwan."

"So you're Chinese?"

"Sure, if you want to write that." Arguing with border guards was almost always pointless. He proceeded to write in his school exercise book that served as the official registry.

I came to Termez because it was to be my springboard into Afghanistan. But Termez had a history of its own. Gan Ying might well have passed through it on his way to Kabul. At the end of the first century and the beginning of the second, when Gan Ying made his journey, Termez was part of the Kushan Empire. The *Hou Han Shu* records Ban Yong, the son of Gan Ying's commander Ban Chao, delivering a report on the Kushan state in 125 A.D. The Chinese, however, continued referring to the country as "Yuezhi," possibly the original name of the confederation of

Indo-European peoples of which Kushan (or "Guishuang" in Chinese records) was one of five branches. Back in the second century B.C., the Yuezhi had been the object of the mission of the explorer Zhang Qian, Gan Ying's great predecessor.

Once again, however, the ancient city that Gan Ying might have seen was no more, destroyed by Genghis Khan. Only a couple of Buddhist ruins lay in the town's environs as testimonies of what used to be.

My entire time in Uzbekistan had resembled the experience of living through a work of surrealist cinema. Now, like a callback to a visual motif from earlier in the film, another oculist's billboard appeared on the dusty road to Termez, a single eye this time staring down at me.

And Marco and Monique followed me here, for no particular reason. I came to Termez to cross the border into Afghanistan. They were supposed to be on their way back to Italy, and Termez was in the wrong direction. They should've been going to Tashkent to catch their flight.

I checked into what was likely the best hotel in Termez, which is not to say that it made do without drab Soviet decor and dark menacing corridors. A handsome young man named Sanja worked the front desk. He turned out to be the proprietor's son who happened to be back from university.

"The Afghan border," I asked Sanja, "how far is it?"

He thought about it for a minute. "Not far. Maybe twenty minutes in a car. You're going to Afghanistan?"

"Yes," I said, "I'll need a taxi to the border tomorrow morning." He nodded in acknowledgement and looked less surprised or shocked than most everyone I had met on this trip when I told them I was going to Afghanistan. For someone from Termez, a stone's throw away from the country that the rest of us had been primed by news reports to fear and to hold in awe, Afghanistan must have seemed like little more than the next neighborhood over. The way a New Yorker might think about Hoboken.

But to me Afghanistan remained a fabled country. And I could just glimpse it from the outskirts of Termez. Shimmering across the Amu Darya in the late-afternoon sun, what I could see of it was no more than an oily-green patch of grassland irrigated by the great river. It was as peaceful a landscape as any that I had ever seen. Deceptively so.

That evening I went through my backpack and threw away things I knew I'd never need in the coming days. In case I had to run for my life, it was better not to be weighed down by unnecessary possessions.

In the morning, I set off to cross the river for the infamous and tragic country on the other side. Surrealism was out. Next up turned out to be a black comedy.

5

HOW I LEARNED TO STOP WORRYING AND LOVE THE PROSPECT OF DEATH

"DO YOU have porno movies?" The Uzbek border official asked, looking at my laptop screen.

"No."

"Seriously, you don't have any porno movies?" He seemed genuinely surprised.

"No, I don't."

"You don't watch movies?"

"You know everything is online now, right?"

He had just finished going over all of the photos on my laptop. Well, not all of them. I had thousands. But at least all the recent ones. He was scrolling up through the pictures from his own country, Kyrgyzstan, and China.

"This is China?" he pointed at one of a pagoda. I told him it was. He kept scrolling, supposedly looking for porn. Then he stopped at another photo. "You have been to Washington?" It was one I took of a hotel where I once stayed on a business trip. The location tag said Washington, D.C.

"Yes, I have."

"Huh."

"I used to work in America," I added but then thought this

was a situation in which I could say too much.

He kept scrolling up and found my photos from trip to Croatia the previous year. "America is a very beautiful country," he sighed with longing.

"That's not America. That's Europe."

"That's not America?" He frowned, surprised. "What country is it?"

"Croatia."

"Where?"

"Croatia. In Europe. You know, used to be Yugoslavia?"

"Whatever." He shrugged, losing interest.

Then he went through my books. He picked up the book that my friend Marina gave me. "To the Ends of the Earth," he read from the cover.

"Yes, it's a travel book by Paul Theroux," I said pointing at the author's name on the cover.

"What's it about?"

"It's a travel book, so basically the author went to a lot of places and wrote about them."

"What places?"

"Well, he took a long train ride from Europe to Asia. So he wrote about that. Hindustan," I adopted their word for India. "China as well. He also went to South America and wrote about that."

"Silk Road?" he suggested, looking for something familiar.

"Sure, there's stuff in here about the Silk Road." I flipped to a page that mentioned Turfan in Xinjiang, China. But the officer had never heard of Turfan and did not know that it fell on the Silk Road as surely as Samarkand.

He had opened my backpack and taken my medicines over to another officer behind a desk. This worried me, because he appeared not to have heard of Ibuprofen and seemed convinced that it was a nefarious narcotic.

"Han, William," the other officer called me over to his wooden desk in the back corner of the room, away from the X-ray machines. The sign on the door read in English, ungrammatically but with paradoxical profundity, "A Hall Is Departure."

All this was taking a great deal of time, but it didn't matter, as I seemed to be the only one crossing the Uzbek-Afghan border on this particular Sunday morning. Actually this wasn't true, as I would spot the occasional Uzbeks in trucks and minibuses, clutching their lime green passports. But right now I seemed to be the only one and not holding anyone up. I kind of wished I were.

"Where are you from?" he asked.

I pointed to the silver lettering on the cover of my passport. "New Zealand."

"But where were you born?"

"Taiwan." Again, I pointed to the readily available information on the biographical page of my passport.

"Thailand?"

"No, Taiwan."

"What is the capital of New Zealand?"

"Wellington."

"No, it's Jakarta."

"No, what? That's Indonesia."

"What's the capital of New Zealand?"

"Wellington."

"Wellington?" He clearly didn't know the correct answer, and the correct answer surprised him with its presumably unfamiliar ring. "Who is the president of New Zealand?"

"There's no president. There's a prime minister."

"Who is the king of New Zealand?"

"There is no king. There is a prime minister."

"Yes, prime minister. Who is it?"

"John Key."

"So who is the head of state there?"

"Well, you see," it occurred to me that, given my personality, the best way to dispel the suspicion that I might be a spy was perhaps to embrace my true nature as a pedant. That and a big smile and a ready laugh. "New Zealand was formerly a British colony. So it inherited from Britain the Westminster parliamentary system, under which we elect a parliament, and a prime minister from parliament. Because it was a British colony and part of the British Empire, the head of state is technically still the queen of England, Elizabeth II."

I flashed a big smile, looking to see how well my lecture on New Zealand government had gone over. But it seemed that I lost him a while back.

"What's the weather like in New Zealand?"

"It's a couple of islands in the ocean, so very different from here."

"Are you married?"

"No."

"Single?"

"Yes."

"Why are you not married?" He gave me a wink full of innuendo. Was this his roundabout way of asking if I was gay? And if I were, what would that mean?

"Just hasn't seemed like the right time."

The other officer, the one who had gone through all my photos, had come over as well. Now he chimed in. "But in the future?" he asked hopefully, for confirmation that I didn't wish to live alone. Suddenly they all seemed very interested in my personal life.

"Yes, in the future."

"What language do they speak in Taiwan?" The first officer resumed his interrogation.

"Chinese, actually."

"What language do they speak in New Zealand?"

"English. And Maori."

"English? Just like in America? Everyone speaks English? Why?"

"Why do they speak English in New Zealand?"

"Yes, why?"

"Well, see, New Zealand was a British colony, so British people went there and settled, so they speak English."

Mr. Porno chimed in again. "Is it the same, the English, in America and in New Zealand?" He seemed genuinely interested as a student of the language.

"It's mostly the same. Some small differences, just habits in how people talk."

"Habits." He ruminated over this.

The interrogator again: "What is the problem with Uzbekistan?"

"Excuse me?"

"You have traveled here. What problems do you see? What is the problem with Uzbekistan?"

Was this an attempt to entrap me into saying something impolitic about his country? "I haven't had any problems," I replied. "Everyone has been very nice to me."

"No, come on. We live here, we know there are problems. Tell us what you think the problems are." Both officers now looked attentively at me.

I thought I'd say something well-acknowledged, if he really needed something from me. "Well, I was in Nukus, and it was a little sad to see the Aral Sea drying up..."

But as soon as I made an earnest answer, he seemed not to

care anymore. "How many countries have you traveled to?"

"In my life?"

"Yes."

"I don't know, thirty-five, thirty-six?" The number provoked a look not so much of suspicion as simultaneously surprise and envy. That number would seem paltry to me in retrospect, before my wandering days would end. But to them, it must have seemed astronomical.

*****

Finally I got my passport back and found my way out of the Uzbek border station. A couple more soldiers with AKs strapped around their torsos stopped me before metal gates painted black and asked to see my passport one last time.

And then before me stood the so-called Friendship Bridge over the Amu Darya, connecting Uzbekistan to Afghanistan. It was perhaps a kilometer long. A train track ran down the middle of it, but no train came. A few desultory trucks and buses had been parked by the Uzbek border post, but none drove my way.

I began walking across it, listening to the sound of my own breathing. I was entirely alone. The shadows of the steel beams holding up the bridge marked my paces like gridiron on a football field. The river, the great Oxus, ran wide and muddy beneath my feet.

One more soldier appeared from a guard post up ahead and came toward me. I took out my passport, expecting one more inspection, but he simply waved me by. I watched his shape grow smaller toward Uzbekistan before turning to resume my solo march.

I came upon an open metal gate at what I took to be the midpoint of the bridge. Here I stopped and surveyed where I was. Uzbekistan behind me now seemed distant. Equally distant on the other side was Afghanistan and the promise of things I could not know to expect.

I was standing atop a major fault line of world history. After the Islamic conquest of the Middle East in the seventh century, the Oxus marked the boundary between Islam and the still pagan Turks, and Arab Muslims would not brave the river in great numbers until over a hundred years later.

When the Soviet Union retreated from Afghanistan, the last soldier to leave, Colonel General Boris Gromov, walked across this bridge in February of 1989 as I was now doing. Only in the opposite direction. I imagined that he stopped roughly where I stood now and turned around to look at the war-ravaged country that he was leaving behind.

Are we doing this?

If a bomb went off and I happened to be passing by, that would be it. If someone pointed a gun at me, I wouldn't be able to wrestle him down like in the movies, because that's in the movies. And if I did wrestle it from him, I wouldn't know how to use it. Once in high school I shot a rifle, and once on a corporate retreat I fired a shotgun at some clay Frisbees. But that was it. I didn't know hand-to-hand combat, save a whole semester's worth of judo in the college gym. And I wouldn't be able to run away, wasn't fast enough. I was never athletic. In high school I played soccer but sucked at it and only played because the school required every kid to play something.

"If I get kidnapped?" I had said to a friend who expressed concern about me going to Afghanistan. "Well, then look for me in an orange jumpsuit on CNN."

The friend let out a series of untranscribable groans.

"Too dark?" I said. "Well, if nothing else, a stay in a cave would be a great weight loss program."

I had registered my travel plans with the New Zealand Ministry of Foreign Affairs, but New Zealand didn't even have diplomatic representation in Afghanistan. I half expected someone from the Ministry to call me and try to dissuade me from going, but no one called. I was almost disappointed.

A couple of days before I crossed the border, I had emailed a select group of friends (my "rescue squad," I said) to apprise them of my plans. I would check in with the group at least once every forty-eight hours, I promised. And if they didn't hear from me, they should, you know, call someone.

These were the people within my social circle who, I thought, might have some relevant connection to be able to pull some strings if something happened to me. A couple of old friends from high school who knew my family and could contact them. A journalist at a major newspaper. A longstanding contributor to the Democratic members of Congress from the State of New York. A corporate attorney who once interned at the Pentagon. A lawyer at the Department of Commerce. And Kathy, an analyst at the CIA.

In response, Kathy sent me the phone number for the U.S. Embassy in Kabul. "After hours," she wrote, "tell the Marine on duty that you want to speak to the duty officer, who is available twenty-four hours a day." Even though I was a New Zealander, she wrote, "they would help you if it were a life-threatening situation." Finally, she added that she would "sleep better" if I were a U.S. citizen. "But if you were, you wouldn't be there anyhow, I suppose."

I looked down at the muddy water beneath the bridge. Then I looked up again at the country a short distance in front of me. There was no turning back now, not in no man's land. No turning back, just as in life, which I supposed was merely a series of no man's lands. I adjusted the straps of my backpack—a stalling tactic, let's admit it. Then I took a deep breath. Life or death, better or worse, here goes.

The first Afghan soldiers I encountered were sitting on the ground at their end of the bridge, leaning against their guardhouse, AKs lying across their laps. Expecting to have to do my time with them, I paused and let out a "*salaam aleikum*." They waved me on.

In the border station, a handsome officer in his thirties wearing military fatigues showed me into his office without even giving me a good look. Only when I handed over my passport with its distinctive New Zealand silver fern on the black cover did he pause and look up.

He opened my passport and saw my visa stamp. "You're a tourist?" he said with incredulity. Before I could decide whether I ought to explain myself, he reached out one hand and bellowed, "Welcome to Afghanistan!"

Well, all right then.

As he took down my information, another officer, a man in his fifties, came into the office as well and gave me an equally warm welcome in equally fluent English. When the younger man finished his work, he showed me into another room directly behind his office. Afghan dishes unfamiliar to me were spread out on the table.

"Please," he gestured at an empty seat. "Eat."

There was a group of them, five or six officers taking their lunch break, sitting together and sharing the food. And now they were all looking at me curiously.

"Well…" I hesitated, feeling incredibly self-conscious under their collective gaze.

"Come! Sit!" They urged me on. I did as I was told and sat down among them. I took up the bread and dipped it in a plate of heavy sauce and green beans. On the side lay chili peppers.

The handsome officer sat down next to me. Seeing that I eyed the chili peppers, he took one and offered it to me. I supposed this to be my first encounter with pashtunwali, the famous Pashtun tradition of hospitality to strangers. But then I remembered that he was almost certainly not Pashtun, not here in northern Afghanistan. Pashtuns mostly lived in the south.

"You're a tourist?" The older officer, who had a wily look about him, asked me as we broke bread. I was about to say yes when he added, "or a terrorist?" Then he burst out laughing, a tinny ring of mania in his voice.

"Don't even joke about that," I said sheepishly.

Then, to my surprised, he switched into Russian. "*Govorish po-Russkiy?*" he asked with a conspiratorial wink, "do you speak Russian?"

I had meant to avoid letting slip any Russian in this country, given the history of the Soviet invasion. But here he was, prompting me. And, even if I failed to reply, the fact that I didn't immediately exhibit the look of incomprehension already answered his question.

"*Nemnogo,*" I said, "some." He nodded and grinned as though to say that we understood each other, though I very much did not understand him.

I wondered what he might have done during the war. Mazar-i Sharif was a major Russian base back then, being only a stone's throw away from Soviet Uzbekistan. And I knew that many Afghans had switched sides depending on which way the wind blew. He had to have been a collaborator during the war, I decided.

Regardless, I appreciated the warm welcome.

When it was time for me to go, he placed his right hand over his heart and tilted his chin ever so subtly to express esteem and to say goodbye. It was a gesture that I came to love in Afghanistan and Iran, a gesture that I came to adopt.

I exited the border station. It was another hour's drive away to Mazar-i Sharif, and the only option was a taxi. Some Afghan cab drivers, however, would drive you straight to the Taliban. I knew this and was standing by the border gate considering my options when a cab pulled up.

The soldier behind me pointed to it and told me, again in Russian, to get in. I decided to accept his endorsement of this particular driver, even as I knew that not every soldier in the Afghan military was trustworthy either. For five tense minutes I sat in the backseat and clutched my belongings as though they contained their weight in gold. Then the driver, an old man with a beard all white, stopped by the side of the road behind half a dozen other parked cars. I poked my head forward, inquiring as to why he stopped. He gestured for me to get out. I did so with apprehension. Half a dozen other men were starting to gather around us. It took me another minute to figure out that they were all taxi drivers as well. It turned out that the old man's job, for one dollar, was only to ferry passengers to the taxi stand of this border town, Hairatan. And one of these guys would now take me into Mazar. I made sure that, when I worked out the situation, none of them heard my sigh of relief.

I struck a deal with one driver, younger but with no less impressive a beard. Less fearful for my life now than a short while ago but far from fully comfortable, I got into his car and headed for Mazar.

*****

On the road into the city the realities of Afghan life unfolded before me. Pickup trucks with machine guns mounted in the back, manned by men wearing red scarves menacingly over their faces, traversed the desert road alongside us. A white jeep marked "UN" idled outside a row of shops. Maimed men missing one leg or both hobbled along on crutches.

Pictures of Ahmad Shah Massoud, the anti-Soviet war hero and Northern Alliance commander assassinated by Al Qaeda, hung over gates and arches and buildings. They showed him in various poses, praying devoutly and looking up toward God, gazing pensively into the distance as though thinking profound thoughts or envisioning his country's future, or looking every bit the romantic soldier and hero. After all, they called him Shir Panjshir ("the Lion of Panjshir").

Sometimes accompanied on the billboards by President Ashraf Ghani and the provincial governor and former warlord Atta Mohammed Nur, Massoud seemed to dwarf both in stature. Which was only natural with the dead and canonized. Political jockeying against martyrs must seem a fool's errand even to the most vainglorious of politicians. No, it was instead a matter of soaking up reflected glory. Did you fight the Russians, Mr. President? No, but my picture is next to someone who did.

It was only an hour but felt like much longer to reach my hotel in Mazar. Time has a way of stretching like a rubber band when you fear for your life.

And when we got there, I saw that it cowered behind a thick wall of concrete, a steel barricade that prevented vehicles from getting too close, and your average guards with AKs. But, catering to international contractors, inside they served German beer. My obvious foreignness served as my pass into the castle keep. The young man at reception, Samir, checked me into my room.

I dropped off my luggage, took a deep breath, and proceeded on a gingerly stroll through the town. Seemingly everywhere armed men stood guard or looked out warily from sniper positions overhead in steel boxes.

The city's central landmark, the twin-domed shrine of Ali, also known as the Blue Mosque, was only a short distance away. The Prophet Mohammed's son-in-law and the inadvertent founder of Shiism (by being murdered while praying) was supposed to have been buried here.

On my way was the ugly fortress that served as the German and Swedish consulates. I say ugly but actually I couldn't see the building proper, hidden as it was behind the high concrete walls and barbed wires rolled out over them like thorns. A quartet of blonde European soldiers stared skeptically at me from behind dark glasses as I walked by. A little closer was an equally heavily guarded structure with posters on the walls of soldiers shot from a low angle and looking heroic. This, I later confirmed with Samir, was an army training center.

The Blue Mosque was an object of great beauty at the heart of this city otherwise host to much ugliness. The turquoise and sapphire tiles, the intricate design of it, came together in a way that did not surpass the great Timurid buildings of Uzbekistan but certainly held its own. The shrine was busy with worshippers: mothers with hijabs over their heads and toddlers in the crooks of their elbows, old men in *shalwar kameez* leaning on their canes.

As an infidel, I wasn't allowed inside the mosque. But the park surrounding it was equally bustling. Men sat around on the blue benches in the shades with their sandals off and their feet on the seats, chatting. On one side the famous pigeons of the shrine fluttered behind a blue steel fence, escaping to fly over our heads and to perch on top of trees. They were all white. The mythology of the shrine held that it was so holy that any pigeon that flew over it turned white instantly.

As the sun began to dip, I looked farther afield to the horizons. The Alborz mountain range lay to the south of Mazar-i

Sharif, an extension of the Hindu Kush. The looming shape of it reminded me of the Ala Archa mountains as seen from Bishkek in Kyrgyzstan. Except no snow capped the Afghan range to make it pleasant and friendly. Instead it was the same dungy color of the desert, harsh as Afghan life itself.

But life went on just like anywhere else. I withdrew my gaze from so far away and found welders and blacksmiths down the street banging on sheet metal and soldering pieces together. Bloody carcasses of cattle hung inside butchers' windows. Electronic stores plied Chinese-made microwaves alongside the same smartphones sold around the world. A banner advertising TOEFL, the English language test for foreign students wanting to study in America, stretched large and optimistic across a thoroughfare.

So, this was Afghanistan.

I lay down on my bed on that first night in-country, closed my eyes, and gave thanks for being alive.

*****

The next morning, young Samir came knocking on my door. "Do you want to go to Balkh now?"

The previous night, as I watched a pair of European contractors nurse the German beer, I had asked him about the possibility of making a trip to this nearby town. Samir spoke the best English among the staff, which made him popular with guests. But he had a kind of insouciance about him that declared that he didn't particularly care for this job and probably much besides. In a different part of the world, you'd expect him to blow off work early to go to an audition for a bit part on the next iteration of CSI.

"I can drive you," he added.

"Right now?" The suddenness took me aback. I had barely finished breakfast.

"Yes, now."

I had wanted to see Balkh because it was the seat of ancient Bactria. In one more claim of Jewish antecedent, some say, very dubiously, that Noah founded the city after the flood. But with or without Noah, the city was very old. It was where Zoroaster or Zarathustra, the founder of Zoroastrianism, preached to his disciples; it was also where he died. The Arabs even called it "the Mother of Cities" in recognition of its antiquity.

Alexander the Great conquered Balkh on his long march to India, taking it after defeating and killing King Bessus of Bactria. Upon entering the city, the Greeks discovered to their horror that the Bactrians left their dead out in the open for wild dogs to consume. Zoroastrian beliefs required the dead *not* to be buried, as doing so would pollute the earth. Zoroastrians also refused to cremate the bodies, as doing so would pollute the air. So dogs were the Bactrian solution to the problem of disposing of the dead, as vultures were in Persia.

Alexander, who up to that point had been remarkably tolerant of cultural differences he found in Asia, finally snapped. He could not abide this funeral by canine mastication. Whatever were his Greek-Macedonian notions of propriety, they only bent so far for the sake of cultural sensitivity. He proceeded to ban the practice of funeral by ritual exposure.

I later came across an interesting essay in *Foreign Policy* magazine by a civilian professor teaching GIs at Forward Operating Base Fenty in Jalalabad, Afghanistan. He recounted an American soldier barging into his classroom one day declaring that he "can't take their shit anymore." By "shit" he meant shit, and by "they" he meant soldiers of the Afghan National Army, who, due to a U.S. policy of winning "hearts and minds," shared latrines with the Americans.

As the professor explained, "it was the custom of the ANA to wipe themselves with their hands, smear their excrement on the walls of the toilette, and rinse their hands in the sink, which left the sinks reeking, a reek made especially acrid and pungent by the Afghans' high intake of goat meat and goat milk."

The professor went on to draw a parallel between the modern Afghan soldiers' personal hygiene habits, which the Americans found so abhorrent, and the ancient Bactrians' disposal of corpses by dogs, which for Alexander was the last straw. How a society deals with waste, the professor explained, whether corpses or feces, is fundamental to its values. And so even culturally sensitive officers going out of their way to accommodate local customs, would-be modern-day successors of Lawrence of Arabia, when directly confronted with a disagreement over how to deal with waste, recoiled in horror.

Horrified as he might have been by their funerary practices, Alexander nonetheless married the Bactrian princess Roxana here, against the advice of his generals. (One wonders whether he ever asked her what was up with their funerals.) After Alexander's death, Bactria became a part of the Seleucid Empire, one of the successor states run by Alexander's generals who divided up the spoils of his conquest. As a result, Bactria remained somewhat Greek.

Gan Ying's famous predecessor in China's western explorations, Zhang Qian, spent time here in Balkh, which he called "Daxia." In his report to the Celestial Court in 126 B.C., Zhang described a populous country with over a million people but without "a great king" and weak militarily, having been defeated by the Kushan, the people whose relics I had examined back in Termez. Zhang was also surprised to find in Daxia products from the Sichuan area in China. The locals told him that these had come via India, evidencing an established trade route.

The Wudi Emperor, in light of Zhang's report, expressed great interest in developing relations with Bactria as well as Persia. By the time Gan Ying came this way at the end of the first century, the Kushan from north of the Oxus had incorporated Bactria into their empire. Subsequently the city became a center of Buddhism. The Tang Dynasty monk Xuan Zang traveled through here in 630 A.D., on his way to India to collect Buddhist sutras to bring back to China. He counted a hundred Buddhist monasteries and three thousand monks in Balkh at that time.

In short, I had to see Balkh.

"Is it safe there right now?" I asked Samir, getting up to go even as I asked.

"Maybe not in the villages, but Balkh itself, yes is okay."

He had wanted to take me in his own car, which he said was a 2007 Toyota Fortuner, specifying the make and model. Indeed, he seemed incredibly proud of the vehicle and wouldn't shut up about it. But somehow the car was not available, and he was vague as to why. So instead he borrowed the car of another hotel employee, an older Toyota, for the trip. Still, Samir kept talking about his car.

"I also go to the gym every day," he added, just so that I'd know.

"You would fit right in in California," I said.

"But it's safe," he reiterated about Balkh. "I took Mr. Joe from the *New York Times* out there a while ago." Samir couldn't remember Joe's last name, but I later inferred that he meant Joseph Goldstein, the Times correspondent in Afghanistan. "Him and these other *New York Times* guys. Two cars, I drove one of them."

He put on some Indian music as the car pulled out and headed west. "Do you like Indian music?"

"I'll listen to whatever you want to listen to," I said.

"I speak Hindi as well as my own language," he added, again just so that I'd know.

It was only a short ride to Balkh. But Samir was right to take what he called a "foreigner car" instead of a "local car," given the bumpy road conditions. But my hopes of finding traces of ancient Bactria were largely disappointed. The old city walls, a Timurid construction, were built on the site of the previous citadel. But the locals, looking for Greco-Bactrian remains as I was, had dug into the mud walls, half tearing them down. So it was that in the Mother of Cities, I failed to come across any specific evidence of its ancient heritage.

Samir drove me to the 1598 shrine of Khwaja Abu Nasr Parsa that formed the center of Balkh, the arteries of which radiated outward from the shrine like a starburst. We got out. As I viewed the shrine, he entered a conversation with a man sitting under a tree. When he was done, Samir reported that the man had warned us that the Bala Hissar ramparts were unsafe to visit. Samir felt it was nonetheless all right to drive out there, as long as I didn't walk around too much.

It was a strange notion being told that the ramparts were unsafe, as they were a mere half mile away from where the advice was being given. If bandits roamed there, wouldn't they be here as well? But when we got out there, I understood a little better. The bustling market that formed central Balkh gave way suddenly to reveal a windswept and deserted plateau. Chunks of the old walls stood here and there on little hillocks. A pair of young boys were playing on one of them to my right. But it was impossible to see over the ones directly ahead, impossible to know who might be behind them. Bandits were known to sweep out from behind there and attack whomever was foolish enough to stand where I stood. Just then one lone motorcyclist appeared out of those hills, riding straight toward me. My hands tightened into fists. But he turned out to be harmless.

"I brought Mr. Joe here, with the other *New York Times* guys," Samir told me when I got back in the car. "Then these cars drove out from up there. And they called me on the phone and said we had to go."

"They were dangerous?"

Samir shrugged. "I don't know. They just said we had to go. Didn't stay to find out."

We proceeded to look for the No Gombad Mosque, a mile south of town in a nearby village. By an intersection Samir pulled up to another man, his faced dark and wrinkled by the sun. When they finished talking, Samir turned to me to announce that, once again, the local security advice was to give the No Gombad a wide berth. Seeing my disappointment, Samir offered to take an alternate route back to Mazar-i Sharif, passing on the way an old mujahedeen base that he promised was worth seeing.

But he just as quickly got lost. The Toyota began winding through some difficult backroads through villages, taking one turn after another, each turn adding to my anxiety. Upon sighting every human male above the age of preadolescence, Samir rolled down his window to ask for directions. Or more accurately, barking for them. And he started swearing when folks told him that it was farther or the way we just came from. "What the fuck," he said again and again in exasperation.

I had no doubt as to Samir's intentions, but I was beginning to doubt his competence. And the way each target of his interrogation looked at me, at the obvious foreigner, the man out of place, made me nervous. I gave each a big smile if he looked at me head on: experience had taught me that people were much less likely to screw you over if they felt a modicum of empathy for you. And then as we pulled away each time a small part of me wondered whether the man we just left behind might pick up his cell and call someone I wished he wouldn't call.

Samir started eyeing me furtively, noticing my nervousness. "Don't worry," he said. "I have gun."

"You do?" *Well, shit, Samir: why didn't you say so earlier? Now I know we have nothing to worry about.*

After a while I asked a follow-up: "What kind of gun?"

"No, no, don't worry," he replied in a non sequitur. "I have gun."

Finally, the potholed village tracks and mud brick houses came to an end, and we were back on some semblance of a road. Samir and I both breathed a sigh of relief.

Then he swore some more. "That fucking guy told me it was just up here, just up ahead." I gathered that he meant the first man who gave him directions, apparently bad ones.

We passed through a township with a chessboard layout, an orderliness that immediately struck me as curious for Afghanistan. "The Russians created this town," Samir explained. "They built it. My girlfriend is from here."

"Really? You want to stop to say hi?"

"No, no, no."

"Are you sure she's not from Canada instead?"

"What?" Samir looked at me in confusion, not understanding the joke of the proverbial Canadian girlfriend.

"Never mind," I shook my head.

"I have had four girlfriends," he offered, again unprompted. "Before, I was very handsome."

I took a second look at his face and mentally shrugged. Before when, I wondered. He was only twenty-three years old.

"Where did you meet them?" I asked.

"In college."

"At what age do people get married around here?"

"Twenty-two, twenty-three," he replied. "But I am not ready for that. When you're eighteen, twenty, you're just a boy, not a man. You don't know what a woman means." I had to concur. "Long live love," read a graffiti on the "cultural center" in the middle of this Russian town.

Finally, we came upon Qal-i Jangi, the mujahedeen base he promised. The name of it, he said, meant "fortress of the hero." The structure looked medieval. But he said it was only a few decades old. "It was a mujahedeen base when the Russians invaded. Then it was a Taliban base. Then it was an anti-Taliban base." Mujahedeen, lest we forget, meant "men of jihad" in Arabic.

"So the Northern Alliance?" I asked, and he confirmed with a nod. "Did Ahmad Shah Massoud fight here, then?" Samir had previously expressed his admiration for the Afghan martyr whose visage seemed everywhere.

"No, he was in Panjshir."

"Ah, right, Shir Panjshir," I said, feeling stupid. Panjshir was over a hundred miles away.

Samir carried on about Massoud the way a novice monk might speak of the patron saint of his order. "He was an engineer, actually. But a real genius. You know, the Russians, when they invaded, they took ninety-five percent of our country. The one place they couldn't take was Panjshir. Panjshir's not so big, not even a province. Just a few mountains. But they couldn't take Panjshir, because of Massoud. They sent three hundred tanks and ten planes but couldn't take it."

In contrast, contemporary politicians left him cold. "We got Ashraf Ghani, he's president, and we got Abdullah, he's president too." Actually, Abdullah Abdullah was the "Chief Executive Officer" of Afghanistan, a position created under American pressure when the election between Abdullah and

Ghani ended in murky controversy. "That's why things are all right in Mazar, because one man is in charge," Samir said, referring to Atta Mohammed Nur, the local strongman. "Same in Herat with Ismail Khan. In Kabul, everyone is in charge, so no one is."

We stopped for one more lingering look at the Qal-i Jangi. The structure would seem romantic to me but for the sense of being rushed, both by Samir and the country of Afghanistan itself. Men with guns stood behind the battlements, dark and menacing figures difficult to make out at this distance. "The police use it now," he added by way of explanation. "Mujahedeen, Taliban, anti-Taliban, now police."

Perhaps it was the thought of Massoud's assassination that put Samir in a gloomy mood. He reflected on his country's recent history and all the killing. "Muslims aren't supposed to kill," he said. "You know in Islam, actually the teaching is that if you kill one person, you kill everyone. You kill everyone in Mazar, everyone in the world. People like DAESH," he said using the Arabic acronym for ISIS, "they are not really Muslims. I think maybe they are from Israel or America."

I tried to ignore this last statement.

*****

The following day I went looking for the Buddhist remnants I missed in Balkh in the somewhat farther town of Samangan. Or more accurately, just outside of it. After two days in Afghanistan, I had grown a little more comfortable, a little more confident that I understood what was happening. Perhaps that was hubris. But in any event, I figured that if I survived one road trip, I could survive another.

Samir's boss Ali, the hotel's proprietor, drove me this time, although Samir came along and snapped photos on his Samsung phone like any tourist. Ali was about my age but—needless to say at this point—looked much older. He didn't speak much English but loved American music. He took a DVD out of the holder above the driver's seat. "He wants to play this for you," Samir explained from the backseat. Ali slipped in the disc. Justin Bieber appeared on the little screen above the player, dancing around, making gestures with his hands meant to be musical. Ali started head-banging. I decided not to tell him that I was not even close to being a Belieber. Next up was Young Dro's "FDB," which stood for a less than decorous sentiment, of which they seemed not at all ignorant.

I asked whether they knew who Springsteen was. They said they did but missed the hint. To the beat of hip hop, and later some saccharine Russian pop, we rode out of Mazar.

And I saw more of the city in the process. A blimp hovered over the airport, an instrument of U.S. military surveillance. Passing a long barb-wired fence that enclosed what seemed like no more than a patch of wasteland, I asked Samir for confirmation of what I figured it was: an abandoned American base.

"They all gone," Samir said, betraying no hints as to how he felt about the Americans' departure.

Then we were on the road to Kabul with the countryside spread out before us. The jagged mountains. The rough-hewn rocks turning red like bloody rust as we went on, streaks of the sanguinary color across the dusty beige and gray. I could easily picture bands of guerrillas squatting up there in the endless rocky pockets, their hands blackened with grime, caressing their best friends the gray metallic barrels. At a moment's notice, they could scramble out of the crevices and attack.

Samangan, in the shadow of the Hindu Kush mountains, was a center of Buddhism under the Kushan. And Takht-i Rostam, which meant "the Throne of Rostam," was in fact a Buddhist monastery, as the stupa indicated. But post-Buddhism, local tradition forgot the place's original purpose and associated the site instead with Rostam, the tragic hero of the Persian epic *Shahnameh*, "The Book of Kings."

Unlike most every other stupa, a mound raised above the earth, this one was carved into the thick rock beneath, in the style of Jordan's Petra. I stood atop the hill out of which the stupa was carved, which overlooked the town in a majestic panorama, a lush green valley huddled between the dry and yellow and barren. A stone building known as a *harmika* atop the stupa once held relics of the Buddha.

The pilgrim was supposed to circumambulate the trench beneath, dug into the earth twenty-five feet deep. So I did the same. Geckos well-adapted to their surroundings kept me company as I made the walk, scurrying in and out of the nooks and crannies. At the foot of the hill, five caves were made in the same fashion out of the same rock face. All of the painted reliefs that would have decorated the chambers of worship and meditation were gone now, defaced by chisels and soot. Or almost all. An enormous lotus flower, that eternal symbol of Buddhist enlightenment, remained on the ceiling of the first chamber but was just barely visible.

Having forgotten the Buddhist association, local tradition now claimed that this was where Rostam married his wife, Tahmina, princess of Samangan. It would have served as an impressive chapel or wedding hall, more impressive still if the old Buddha statues remained in their niches. A beam of sunlight shone through the oculus by the lotus, catching the dust that we had kicked up, as though suspending the specks in midair, a literal image of enlightenment. Oculi in the next caves achieved a similar effect. Two vaulted galleries with their carved windows filtering in the same sunlight reminded me instead of a faraway place: a corner of Gaudi's Park Güell in Barcelona.

I returned to Mazar-i Sharif with Bamiyan on my mind, dreaming of the giant Buddha statues that stood there until the Taliban put dynamites under them and lit the fuse.

*****

That afternoon I went shopping for an Afghan outfit for the sake of blending in. I never played dress-up traveling in foreign countries, but for once I would make an exception. As far as Afghanistan went, Mazar was about as safe as it got. But I was going to Kabul next, and I needed a disguise. A traditional shalwar kameez with the balloonish pantaloons were just the thing, plus a scarf as every Afghan man wore it.

A row of shops, some selling clothes, stood just across the street from my hotel. At the first shop I stepped into, the shopkeeper with a guilty grin asked for twenty dollars for the ensemble. Guilty because even he knew how ridiculous that price was by Afghan standards. I gave him a "c'mon man" look and went to the next shop.

Two boys were working here, one maybe sixteen or seventeen, the other maybe fourteen and already sporting a downy mustache, but he looked like he would have been cherubic at a younger age. The gray shalwar kameez I liked was two sizes too small, so I had to settle for a rusty brown combo and a black-and-white checkered scarf. The boys asked for eight dollars for the lot.

By this time, I had caused a small commotion on this busy street lined with shops, and a half dozen guys were staring at the foreigner buying clothes. I paid the boys, took a photo with them, and escaped back to the hotel to try on my new gear.

*****

I had arrived in Afghanistan at a bad time, if there was ever such a thing as a good time. Two and half weeks earlier, news broke that Mullah Omar, head of the Taliban, had in fact died in 2013. Thereafter Mullah Akhtar Mohammed Mansour became the new leader. Presumably because the new leader now had something to prove, the Taliban then carried out a series of bombings in Kabul while I was admiring madrasas in Uzbekistan.

The day before I walked across the Friendship Bridge, the U.S. Embassy in Kabul issued a warning that insurgents were planning to attack several targets in the city over the next few days. On my second day in Mazar-i Sharif, a German citizen was kidnapped in Kabul.

And the third day after my border crossing, when I was planning on going to Kabul, happened to be Afghanistan's independence day. It was on August 19, 1919, that Afghanistan signed an agreement with Britain, which granted Afghanistan its independence — which was strange because Afghanistan was never *not* independent, never part of the British Empire. No matter, August 19, when I was supposed to get to Kabul, was a symbolic date and thus invited attacks. I decided to delay my arrival by one day.

I did the cold calculus of life and death in my head: If, in a city of three and half million, ten people were killed or kidnapped on an average day, then the chances of getting killed or kidnapped after spending one day in the city was one out of 350,000. Suppose a foreigner was a hundred times more likely to be a victim, that still left me with a probability of one out of 3,500, or only about 0.03 percent each day. Tolerable odds for a brief stay.

To get to Kabul, I accepted the vague ignominy of air travel, that bending of the human sense of space and time evolved from eons when we could travel no faster than we could run. Samir had said that the road from Mazar to Kabul was safe enough, but the Afghan consul in Bishkek had begged to differ. And it was a nine-hour drive, during which anything could happen. And I didn't have money to hire armed escorts. In this instance, I agreed that discretion was the better part of valor.

Kam Air greeted me with a grammatically dubious slogan: "Trustable Wings," which made me wonder whether its pilots' skills were any less dubious. And the plane was a Ukrainian hand-me-down, which again failed to inspire confidence.

The U.S. military, in fact, briefly blacklisted Kam in 2013 for opium smuggling. Also, Kam Air supposedly helped Hamid Karzai's brother spirit out of the country the billion dollars he stole from the defunct Kabul Bank. Two million dollars on each flight to Dubai, hidden in the trolleys of soft drinks that the stewardesses pushed down the aisles. But the airline had politically connected friends, and the U.S. dropped it from the blacklist.

Flying had its own reward, though. From the air, an hour after dawn, the morning light beaming from the eastern horizon bisected the mountain tops of northern Afghanistan, like a scalpel, into the dark and the bright. And the bright was so bright and the dark so dark in contrast that the latter seemed not to exist at all except only as lacunae. The patches of black looked like jagged rips in the fabric of the world. And if the plane nosedived into one of them, then it would surely not crash but instead fall into some twilight zone, some alternate dimension.

A soldier was sitting a few rows in front of me. One shoulder patch read "NATO—Resolute Support." The other read, "Croatia," with the red-and-white shield of the coat of arms of that country.

And sitting next to me was a kindly, older man with a beard

all turned white wearing the shalwar kameez. A couple of times he turned to look at me, with obvious interest, and I just smiled. Then he began talking to me. He said he was a doctor working for the government, and it was his job to fly into Mazar every once in a while to inspect the health of the local prison population. He asked me what I was doing in Afghanistan. "Working? Doing research?"

"I guess I'm sort of doing research." Briefly I explained Gan Ying's mission to Rome.

He nodded, somehow not surprised, which surprised me. "And you'll write about it?"

"I'll try." Then I added, "I suppose that makes me also a kind of tourist." Usually I loathed associating myself with that word, conjuring as it did for me gauche ignoramuses climbing out of tour buses in board shorts and silly hats, waiting for their guide to tell them what to see and when to eat lunch.

But in Afghanistan, or at least at its northern border crossing and in Mazar-i Sharif, the word seemed to carry a strange and unlikely magic. Everyone in Mazar seemed elated upon hearing the word "tourist."

Samir explained it to me this way: "Because tourists don't come to get anything. They come, they see, they take pictures, they go."

I supposed it must be refreshing not to deal with people with agendas, even altruistic ones, the journalists and the contractors and the bureaucrats and the military types and the do-gooders. And, I thought, perhaps the word "tourist" also carried with it a kind of normalcy that they so craved. Normal countries have tourists. War zones have journalists and aid workers.

I asked the old doctor for his thoughts on Farah in southwestern Afghanistan. In Gan Ying's day it was called Alexandria Prophthasia, or *Wuyishanli* in the Chinese transliteration of the time. The *Hou Han Shu* clearly mentioned it as a part of his journey. I very much wanted to go there if I could.

There was only one small difficulty: it was crawling with Taliban.

"Farah? Yes, it's very nice," said the old man.

"Very nice?" I had been taking an unscientific poll on Farah, and this was the first time anyone described it this way.

He shrugged. "It's beautiful."

"Is it safe to go?" I asked. Samir and everyone else had answered this question in the negative.

"Yes, it is safe," he said brightly like a travel agent trying to sell a package tour. "You can fly there."

"Is it?" I was surprised to hear this contrarian answer.

"Well, okay, what is safe anyway?" He turned up the palms of his hands. "You can get hit by a car anywhere. There are murderers and kidnappers everywhere."

"Umm…" Under different circumstances, I might enjoy such a philosophical debate. But when it came to the question of the prospect of my own death, I preferred to keep the discussion entirely pragmatic.

"I mean," the old man added, "Kabul is not safe."

Terrific.

*****

He was not wrong. Kabul, at the precise juncture when I arrived, was a city under siege. Mazar-i Sharif, where my hotel made do with one guard at the door with one assault rifle, one steel barrier against vehicles, and one steel gate, was child's play in comparison. In Kabul, a city rocked by the recent series of bombings, every security measure multiplied.

When I arrived at my hotel there, I found three separate

barriers guarding against car bombs. Having proceeded past those followed by half a dozen armed guards, I entered a steel corridor that led up to the entrance of the hotel. The corridor was divided into thirds, and the doors between the three compartments only opened when the guard on one side knocked, and the guard on the other side verified through a peep hole that it was his counterpart doing the knocking.

In the first compartment, a pair of guards greeted me. I said I had a reservation. They let me into the second compartment, which turned out to be built as a Faraday cage, so that no cell signal was available inside it. Another pair of guards waited for me here, next to a metal detector. I said I had a reservation.

"What company?" one of the guards, a man with so much weariness in his face that I felt exhausted just looking at him, asked me.

"I'm not with any company," I said. "I'm just me."

This response deeply confused him. No one came here independently.

"I have a reservation," I added hurriedly. "I emailed the reservation desk and received a confirmation."

"What is your name?" he asked.

I told him.

"Show me your passport."

I handed it over. He picked up the phone on the wall and presumably dialed reservation. "You're not on the list," he said when he hung up. "You can't come in."

This was troubling.

"Look," I said, "I can show you the email confirmation." I had my phone in my hand and now waved it around pathetically.

He understood, though. "Go back," he said. "You can get signal in the previous room."

That made sense. The previous compartment was not a

Faraday cage like this one, and cell signals could go through. I picked up my backpack again and retreated into the previous compartment. It worked.

When I was able to return to prove to him that I had a reservation, he went through all my luggage, thoroughly. Finally, they showed me into the third compartment and into the hotel lobby, hidden behind the fortress.

*****

I had an epiphany about the Afghan hotel.

Hotels aren't usually very interesting subjects. Their function and their workings are basically always the same and always mundane, only different hotels accomplish their purposes with different degrees of success and flare.

But my Kabul hotel was unlike any other where I had stayed. Other hotels' primary function was to ensure the guests' comfort and to make them feel welcome and able to do what they had to do or wished to do. This hotel's primary function was to assure its guests that they would not die here. It was a suit of armor. Everything inside the hotel was to be defended by this armor, and everything outside of it was a threat that the armor was meant to protect against.

But as much as actually serving as an armor, the hotel's purpose was also to endow its guests with the feeling of wearing this armor. This was the chief product that this hotel, and presumably other Kabul hotels, sold. Attributes that, at any "normal" place of accommodation, would be considered bugs were here features.

Most obviously, the inconvenience of heavy security checks and pat-downs and going through four sets of steel doors each time one went outside, even if literally just poking one's head out to see whether the taxi had arrived, was a necessity. But an insufficiently inconvenient hotel would also seem insufficiently secure and thus fail to deliver the service it promised. It was not unlike building an impractical and impedimental wall around one's country: Whether the wall actually did anything was secondary to the builders being able to point to it and say, "Look! We built a wall! We're keeping you safe!"

Plastered all over the interior of the building were notices stating, "No Photography!" There was a practical justification in preventing the photographing of security measures, but these notices were so ubiquitous as to demand that nowhere inside the hotel was ever photographed. Not the garden courtyard, not the divans in the lobby, not the balcony outside the restaurant on the top floor. Even though an entire photo gallery appeared on the hotel's own website, displaying all the "No Photography!" areas for all to see. The purpose of preventing guests from taking photographs was therefore specifically to inconvenience them in a specific way that palliated their fear of their own mortality. It's a security measure, you see!

After a while, even the bad food — the immutable breakfast of greasy sausages and very English baked beans with plasticky hard-boiled eggs and instant coffee made with lukewarm water with chunks of powdered milk floating in it like sewage scum — felt like a feature and not a bug. The prison quality of the food served as a reminder that none of us was ready to die, definitely not here, that there were finer things to live for: a properly cooked steak, a real bottle of Bordeaux, a breezy summer evening on Lake Como. If you give up the ghost in this town, the food seemed to be saying to the guest reluctantly swallowing this garbage, then I will be the last meal you ever put in your mouth, and do you really want that? Like, seriously?

I wondered about the other guests staying here. I was a mere traveler, and I seemed clearly to be the only one. Everyone else I kept seeing at breakfast seemed a journalist or an NGO type. What journalism could anyone do encased in this armor all the time? How would any development specialist or policy advisor understand from inside these walls the country outside that the policy advice was supposed to be about?

Gan Ying took much greater risk to get here, I told myself. Sure, there was no ISIS back then and no truck bombs. But there were also no reliable maps, no planes, no phones, no Internet, no trains or cars, and no idea where the hell he was going. Modern criminals and terrorists could pose no more danger than ancient highway banditry along the Silk Road.

And what of the city that he would have found? The *Hou Han Shu* called Kabul "Jibin." And it would have been part of the Kushan Empire. The Kushan prince Kujula Kadphises united the five tribes of Yuezhi and, according to another section of the *Hou Han Shu*, conquered Kabul around 45 A.D. The Sassanians of Persia would not arrive to defeat the Kushan until the 3rd century.

*****

I put on my Afghan outfit and came back down to the lobby. It worked well enough to half-conceal my identity and make me feel clever. Afghan men often wore scarves over their heads to shield them from the scorching sun. The scarf in my case neatly covered my face unless looked upon straight on. This, I felt, was going to help to keep me safe.

The woman working at the reception desk was the one who had previously checked me in. She was a cheerful, somewhat corpulent woman in her thirties. And she seemed impressed by my outfit.

"You look Afghan," she said. "Hazara, actually. You know Hazara?"

The Hazara were an ethnic minority group in Afghanistan descended from the Mongols who followed Genghis Khan to this country.

"Yes, I know," I said, still feeling self-congratulatory.

"You know DAESH?"

"Yes, I know," I said again.

"They like to kill the Hazara," she said.

"Wait, what?"

"DAESH. They like to kill the Hazara, because they are Shiites."

"Well," I sighed with resignation. "Shit."

I asked her about going out to see something of Kabul. She insisted that local yellow cab drivers couldn't be trusted with not kidnapping me. She would call the taxi company with which the hotel had a contractual relationship and get a reliable driver.

Twenty minutes later the driver came. He spoke surprisingly good English. Later he explained to me that his uncle was a wealthy doctor and spent his money on education for his sons and nephews. He mentioned that he was Hazara himself, and I thought with mild alarm that we bore no resemblance to each other whatsoever. But it didn't matter now that I knew that the Hazara also had targets on their backs.

He also told me that I looked all right in my new get-up. "But next time," he said pointing at my North Face day bag, "leave the backpack."

I asked him to take me to Babur's Garden, built by that founder of the Mughal Dynasty in India, and then the old city walls. Here was my first, modestly frightened, chance to see modern Kabul.

The city stretched out toward the mountains on all sides that marked its geographical and human boundaries, like honey in a shallow bowl, the porcelain edge tapering upward to contain the thick, sticky fluid within that would keep spreading if you let it. But what the bowl contained was not honey, nothing nearly so sweet.

It was a city on edge, reeling from a series of bombings that had killed dozens just days earlier. It was a city divided, between the foreign and the Afghan, between the rich and everyone else. It was a city half-crazed with fear and the injustice of chance, of fate, of being in the wrong place at the wrong time. I imagined that Saigon circa 1973 might have felt a bit like this.

My driver was disparaging of the Americans. "They said they were going to fix Afghanistan. Now they're leaving, and Afghanistan is not fixed." The Obama administration had announced its plans for withdrawal by the end of the year. "The Taliban controls eighty percent of the country…"

"Eighty percent?"

"Sure. The government controls only the cities. The countryside is all Taliban."

"In fairness to the Americans, they have been here for fourteen years. How much longer do you want them to stay?"

"That's true, they have been here a long time."

To my embarrassment, I got all Chinese on him. "Here's what I'd say as a Chinese person. Only the Chinese could save China." I was referring to, and giving a very compressed and not at all consensus view of the civil war of 1945-49, after which U.S. politicians would accuse each other of "losing China."

"It was foolish and ridiculous for anyone to count on the Americans to come in and rescue us," I went on tendentiously. "So I say only the Afghans can save Afghanistan. This is true with any people: they are the ones they have been waiting for. Always."

"Yes," he said with a dreamy sigh, "everything is good in China now. You have power, you have good lives…"

"I don't know about everything…" Also, I didn't live there, never had. But I chose not to mention this fact.

"But it's so good there."

"It's a lot better than it used to be, sure. But it took decades. And you know, millions of people died in the process."

He kept telling me that I couldn't go here or go there. The old citadel walls, for example. "You have to go through the local neighborhood to get there," he said, "and you really shouldn't."

"Oh, come on," I said. "I really would like to see the citadel."

"Look," he pleaded, "when they kidnap a foreigner, the first thing they do is shoot the driver." It seemed impossible to argue with that, so I let the matter drop.

At Babur's Garden, he rushed me past scenes of families enjoying an afternoon outdoors and points of interest like Babur's sarcophagus, begging me not to take pictures in a public place for fear of drawing attention. "Okay? Okay?" he kept asking, prompting me to get going.

Only later did I learn from my expat contact Janhavi that it was the Afghan way always to say no, and it was up to the guest to push back and to insist. "The only time you have to back off is if they say you'll die," Janhavi said to me. "That's when you know they really mean it."

Not only that, but the young man who worked reception at my hotel turned out to go out of his way to feed me bad information.

I had wanted to make a stop in Bamiyan, where the massive Buddha statues that Xuan Zang described in the seventh century once stood. (Tantalizingly, Xuan Zang also described a third, even bigger, reclining Buddha, which had yet to be discovered.) The Taliban dynamited them when they were in power. But the empty niches carved into the mountains still looked over the land, judgmental of man's folly. And nearby the half dozen sapphire lakes of Band-i Amir formed Afghanistan's first national park.

Overland travel was considered too dangerous now, given sporadic fighting along the way. How about flying?

"The airport in Bamiyan is closed for the rest of the month," the young man told me. For one day I believed him with disappointment. Then I inquired with travel agents. Uniformly they told me that this was crazy talk. But there were only two flights a week, and the next flight by now was fully booked.

I came back to the hotel quite angry with the misinformation. "No, it is closed, I swear," he doubled down. "I'll call my travel agency." After a minute on the phone, he hung up to repeat the falsehood.

A similar thing happened when I went to the Kabul Museum. I asked for a car to take me there. "The museum is closed today, holiday." It was a Friday, the equivalent of a Sunday in a Muslim country, it was true. But I had been given no uncertain advice that the place was open on Friday mornings. I asked him if he could confirm by calling the museum. "No, this is Afghanistan, you cannot call. They don't have phones."

"The museum has no phones?"

"No phones."

"Does it have a website that you can check?" I asked.

"No."

"Let me Google that for you." Sure enough, not only did the museum have a website, the website had a phone number on it, and it also had operating hours. "See, it's open."

He turned angry, as though he were the schoolmaster and I some unruly pupil who had disputed his authority. "You should have come to me with this information earlier."

"It's your job to help me!" I bellowed with exasperation. "Not the other way around!"

Finally, he agreed to call a car. By the time it arrived, the museum was actually approaching closing time, so I told the driver to forget about it. The next day when the receptionist called the cab company again, he made sure to tell them that I canceled on them the last time so they should charge me double.

I began to sympathize with Gan Ying on a new level: When he reached the Persian Gulf, confronted with water, he asked the local fishermen for advice on how to reach Rome. They told him that he had to sail around the Arabian Peninsula to Egypt, and that the voyage would take three years. This was very misleading advice. The Levant was a Roman province at the time. To reach the Roman Empire from the Persian Gulf, Gan Ying only needed to traverse Mesopotamia. The route would have been direct and not even all that long.

Even more incredibly, the Persians told him that demons haunted the seas, female demons who sang songs to sailors so that they forgot their homelands — i.e., the Sirens from Homer's *Odyssey*. A tall tale borrowed from the Greeks and sadly believed by a man from inland China who had no experience with the ocean.

These same Persian fishermen, I thought, could easily be the ancestors of my pathological liar hotel receptionist. In my mind's eye, I pictured some Persian or other, looking rather like this young man, saying to Gan Ying, "No, Mister, cannot go, road closed, no road, desert, you die. Must get boat, sail around. Three years. But lady demons sing songs and take your soul."

Historians have speculated that the Persians lied to Gan Ying to prevent him from reaching Rome because they held a middleman's monopoly in the silk trade. If the producers (the Chinese) made direct contact with the consumers (the Romans) then they could have cut out the middlemen. And the Romans would have found out how much the Persians had been gouging them.

Looking at my receptionist, I wondered whether historians gave the fishermen too much credit. Could they not have lied just for the amusement, as my man seemed to be doing to me? What benefit did he gain by preventing me from doing what I wanted to do? Perhaps the Chinese failed to meet the Romans when both empires were at the height of their powers, perhaps world history turned out this way, for no better reason than that some guy living on the Persian Gulf at the time for no particular reason decided to lie to a stranger from a faraway land and have some fun at his expense.

Later it occurred to me that it made sense for the hotel staff to discourage its guests from escaping the protection of the armor, what the hotel was selling. "It's closed," "It's not safe," "I don't think you should go." The message was always the same: you are wearing an armor, our armor, and it is ridiculous ever to take it off. Because if you ever take it off, you'll probably die. It made a kind of messed up sense for them even to lie to me to make sure that I never went anywhere and never did anything.

Two Afghan women were sitting in the lobby and overheard me asking about Bamiyan. The receptionist told me that the woman in her twenties was a lawyer, and the middle-aged woman a judge. I said I was a lawyer as well. The young man claimed to be a law student. The two women asked why I wanted to go to Bamiyan. The question surprised me, as Bamiyan was the crown jewel of Afghan tourism before the war — of course, back then there were actual Buddha statues to see.

"It's not obvious why I want to go?" I answered rhetorically.

"I think," said the judge, "if DAESH catch you, they kill you."

She was laughing, as was her younger associate. High-pitched, grating laughs, laughs with their incisors. Not only with their mouths but with their eyes as well. That contempt for the

171

ridiculous in their eyes.

"What do you do if DAESH get you?" she added.

I shrugged and turned up my palms. Sure, there would be little I could do if that happened. They laughed some more.

"Let us exchange," said the lawyer.

"I don't understand," I said. "What do you want to exchange?"

My mendacious receptionist joined in this discomfiting comedy.

"They say you can stay here in Afghanistan if you like it so much," he said. "And they will go live in China. How is that?"

Of course they assumed I lived in China. The lot of them seemed to think that a foreigner who actually came to their country and wanted to experience something of it had to be some sort of a jester or a fool.

*****

I went to see my contact Janhavi. She wore her own sort of armor. Janhavi was a developmental specialist from India and worked for one of the NGOs within the Aga Khan network. A mutual friend in New York had introduced us virtually as I was cleaning out my apartment on Twenty-Seventh Street. She invited me over to meet her friends.

She shared a nondescript house with a vegetable garden with an Englishman, Nick, and an American woman Lisa from northern Virginia. The house was only a stone's throw from my hotel, but still the recommended mode of travel was by taxi. I ignored this advice and put on my Afghan get-up. As usual, it took me ten minutes just to get past the security and out of the building. On my way out, the receptionist laughed at what he perceived to be my inexplicable affection for Afghan fashion, or affectation.

Google Maps said it was a ten-minute walk, but it felt a lot longer. In the waning light of late afternoon, I kept looking over my shoulders like a suspicious wolf as I walked. The streets were mostly deserted. But anyone who came into striking distance of me in my disguise I scrutinized surreptitiously. No one gave me a second glance—unless the kidnappers were just that good.

Janhavi's security guard, a muscular middle-aged man and veteran of the Soviet war, opened the door when I arrived. With his vigilant eyes he puzzled over this strange, perhaps comical apparition.

"Yes?" he said with a gruff, gravelly voice, no doubt ready to take me down even with his bare hands.

"Hi!" I said brightly, stupidly. "I'm here to see Janhavi."

"And who are you?"

How could I explain this, I wondered. Who am I indeed. As I opened my mouth again to try to string together a coherent answer, Janhavi appeared behind the guard.

"It's all right," she said. "He's here to see me."

The guard tossed me one last suspicious glare before stepping aside. Janhavi looked me up and down. "Not bad," she said, referring to my outfit. "For a second, I wondered who is this Afghan guy at the door."

As we chatted, I told her about my conversation with the Hazara driver about Americans leaving the Afghans in a lurch.

"The Americans did a lot for Afghans," she said with indignation at the injustice. "Sure, they made a lot of mistakes, but they also did a lot to help. Also, when Americans were here in force, all that the Afghans said was that the Americans were the cause of the problems. That the Taliban wouldn't be attacking if there were no Americans here. Now the complaint is that they're leaving, which is exactly what the Afghans said they wanted. And all the Afghans I work with are now asking me to help them with asylum applications. They all want to leave."

The image of rats scuttling off a sinking ship appeared in my mind.

Janhavi offered me a drink. "There's not much to do here but to drink, because often you can't go out at night. Something to take the edge off. And you're limited to two bottles when you carry alcohol into the country, so you're not going to carry wine or beer, always liquor. For a while bottles were practically falling off the backs of NATO trucks, so now it's not just expats but Afghans too who drink. Really, everyone here is drinking too much."

I had expected a dry couple of weeks in Afghanistan, but instead I got a hangover.

Other friends of theirs showed up. Simona from Romania and Mariam, the only Afghan among us and ethnically a Tajik. They brought a bottle of tequila.

Lisa from Virginia was a reedy, beautiful brunette with delicate and innocent features, chief among them a perky nose. She now worked for the American University of Afghanistan. She asked me how old I was. I brought out the old saw about being the same age as Jesus upon crucifixion.

"So, thirty-three," she replied.

I laughed. "You must be Catholic?"

"My mom was a nun," she said also with a laugh. "She divorced God."

Lisa had twice survived attacks unscathed, one bombing and one shooting. The hotel just in front of their house was the scene of a shooting by a trio of gunmen only three months earlier that killed fourteen people. It was closed for business for now. And just the other day, young men with walkie-talkies waited for her outside her office, casing the joint as it were.

"Don't you have security?" Janhavi asked. Her former boss, a

Frenchman, was kidnapped once and held for seventy-five days. Quietly the organization paid a five-million-dollar ransom out of a development grant from the German government under a deal in which the French government then reimbursed the fund. Meanwhile the Allied nations continued to spout the official line about never negotiating with terrorists.

"Clearly they're useless," Lisa concluded.

They had little confidence in the security men who were meant to advise them.

"Our guy," Janhavi was saying, "is just sending us postings on Kabul Security Now," a Facebook group. "Or messages from Nasim Beg," another supposed security expert. "But I'm already on Nasim Beg's mailing list. So I literally get no new information from him. It's the same stuff on Kabul Security Now, which is usually just rumors anyway. And the postings appear between bestiality videos that some douchebag keeps putting up."

But Nasim Beg was an Ismaili, they noted, and membership in that minority Islamic sect was enough to make him a diversity hire in Afghanistan.

"Nasim Beg keeps asking me about Christina Kim," Lisa said, referring to a former roommate. "He thinks I still live with her. She left three years ago. But every time I see him, he's like, 'How's Christina? You're living at that house, right?' I'm like, 'no.' But next time it's the same thing." It seemed bad that the "security expert" couldn't retain any new information.

"Here's the thing," Janhavi said to me, "they know who I am," referring to the bad guys. "They know where I live, they know where I work, they know my routines. If they want to kidnap me or kill me, they can. They have a thousand opportunities. People say vary your routines. But how much can I actually vary my routines? I have to be at work by a certain hour. So at most it's the difference between leaving home at 7:30 and leaving at 8:30. All they have to do is wait an hour. If they want to get me, they can."

"The way it works with kidnappings," she went on to explain for my benefit, "is that usually your kidnappers are just some criminals. Then they give you seventy-two hours for your organization to negotiate your release. If that doesn't happen, then they sell you to the Taliban. The Taliban then demands a ransom, naming the price based on your nationality and which organization you work for." It all sounded to me a bit like insurance companies or personal injury lawyers calculating the correct compensation for a severed thumb or a lost foot.

One of their friends had died the previous week.

Not a bombing, not a killing, nothing that one associated with living in a war zone. A hiking accident. A slip of the foot, and down the cliff he went. That was that. In Band-i Amir, the national park. One got so used to contemplating the fiery potentialities of death in a conflict zone that a mundane way to go seemed bizarre, nonsensical, incomprehensible. Was it supposed to be funny? How could something that could have happened anywhere happen in a place where nothing normal was supposed to happen? Tears bubbled in Lisa's eyes when she talked about the lost friend, and Janhavi got choked up as well.

"You must think I'm either foolish or crazy to have traveled here without having to," I said.

"We're all crazy here," Simona chimed it, wisely. "We all chose to come here. Most people wouldn't have. You just did it under different circumstances than we did." There was indeed a faint sense of madness in the air, a silent laughter born of a killing joke.

It was true that they had all come here voluntarily. It was also true that they were now all trying to get out. Somehow. Sooner rather than later. "It's just too much," Simona said. Janhavi spoke of her plans of escape, of finding a different job somewhere more comfortable, like Thailand.

"But you know you'll come back here," Simona pointed out. Her friend paused for a moment before conceding the point. Kabul, Afghanistan, seemed to have grown inextricably part of each of them, and they knew it, which was perhaps not surprising when the relationship they had with this city and this country was one of such intensity. You could get the NGO worker out of Kabul, but you couldn't get Kabul out of the NGO worker.

Nick now came home. He was late, having played soccer at the British Embassy. A classic English lad with somewhat crooked teeth and British good cheer, he seemed not to share the women's gloom. And when the four women began exchanging stories of harassment by Afghan men, neither of us had much to add and could do no more than listen incredulously to the foolishness of some of our fellow men:

"This guy kept calling me and calling me, from nine different numbers..."

"This guy called and pretended to be a woman, and I was like, 'Uh, I can tell you're a man, and a woman doesn't sound like that at all...'"

"These boys reached under our burqas and grabbed our asses..." Sometimes they needed burqas to get around. Other times a hijab sufficed.

Janhavi: "Or like Dr. Nasruddin—doctor, yeah—saying that there were no rapes under the Taliban because there were no rapes reported."

Lisa: "This guy called me and said, 'I make you my wife.' Next time he called and said, 'I fuck you.' Third time he called and said, 'I kill you.'"

Simona: "Some guy wrote me a poem about the river of love, or something. It was poetic."

Mariam: "I made a guy shut up once. I told him I had contacts in the police and that they would trace his number and track him down."

The Afghan cell phone carrier Roshan had a calling plan offered only to women called the "princess" plan. "You can block up to five numbers for free," Mariam explained for my benefit.

Perhaps it was all no worse than some messages that women anywhere received on Tinder. But I had always suspected that terrorism was fundamentally a Freudian matter, of frustrated male sexual energy sublimated in a peculiarly unproductive way. If everyone got laid and didn't have to feel guilty about it, at least not religious guilt, then men would all find better ways to spend their time than blowing themselves up.

One expat party in Kabul was surreal enough. But somehow we managed to do it again the next night. I walked the same route, more certain of my way now but no less looking over my shoulders.

Australian Jon showed up, rectifying the gender balance a little. He was from outside Sydney but lived in Scotland when he wasn't in Afghanistan. He was athletic with a tattoo on his right forearm, wore glasses, and sported a European comb of the hair to one side. Politically conservative, he worked for a French consultancy that did analysis work including for the U.S. military. And he just so happened to love the oeuvre of Taylor Swift. Most everyone in his firm, though, was about to leave Afghanistan or had already left in light of the recent bombings. Sitting with him in the enclosed yard, I asked him what sort of analysis he did.

"We call it 'atmospherics,'" he replied with proud vagueness.

"What you do," Nick chimed in with friendly sarcasm, "is you aggregate everything from the Internet and conclude that there's a war going on."

Nick started talking about the NDS, National Directorate of Security, Afghanistan's leading security and intelligence agency alongside the CID, the Criminal Investigation Department of the national police.

"It's the only somewhat competent agency here," he said. "Too bad it's also utterly corrupt. Coming from the Embassy right now, I see these NDS guys in their car parked outside. They're just kids, teenagers. And they're smoking hash in the car. Completely high. I walk past them and they're like, 'ho-ho-ho,'" he did his best impression of a stoned teenager on his parents' couch, amused by some cartoon comedy on TV.

We were back in the living room now and pouring each other glasses of gin and tonic. Janhavi told Nick about my plans for writing this book. I said apologetically that perhaps it was presumptuous of me, as I was clearly little more than a tourist in Afghanistan, a country in which I had no expertise.

"But a savvy one," Janhavi said, again to my gratification. "A few months ago," she went on, "there were these French girls here. Two girls. They went around Kabul dressed like they would in Paris. Officers from the French embassy came and swept them off the street, stuck them on a plane headed for Charles de Gaulle, because there had been so much chatter that they were about to get kidnapped."

Now I felt less complimented, if the bar for savviness was so low.

Nick got suddenly serious. "I'm a tourist," he said, "just like you." He had been living in Afghanistan for the last two years and certainly spoke a lot more Dari than I did. "I don't understand this country. You know someone is full of shit if he says he understands Afghanistan. The guy who's been here two weeks is like, 'Here's the thing about the Afghans.' The guy who's been here ten years says, 'I don't know anything.'"

Nick respected Rory Stewart, the British politician and author of *The Places in Between*, which chronicled his walk from Kabul to Herat in 2002. "Because he says he doesn't understand the Afghans," Nick said. "He was only recording what happened with him, even though he was actually fairly expert on the subject, speaking Dari and all. You take something like *Three Cups of Tea*, on the other hand," the much-critiqued account of Greg Mortenson's humanitarian efforts in Afghanistan and Pakistan. "It's total bullshit, totally romanticizing."

"No one believes in what they do here," Janhavi said to me. "It's all political, all donor-driven. You might see a problem that you want to solve, but you can't actually just go and solve it. You have to do what the system allows you to do, and you try to make it as close to what you really want to do as possible. Then you justify your work to yourself, saying that there is value in it. But the truth is — Lisa can tell you this, she works in monitoring and assessment — there is no way to prove that a program helps anyone.

"Let's say you put together an educational program. You can assess how many girls and how many boys you enroll in the schools. But you can't measure how many of their families are threatened because they're sending their daughters to school. You can't measure how many families are going into poverty trying to pay the school fees. So what do you do when you're supposed to assess the program's success? You just write your own criteria and focus on the things you want people to focus on. You write the test that you give yourself, so of course you pass with flying colors. That's development work."

And then, she added, there was the way people competed for money and prestige just as though they were in the for-profit sector. "It's like the mean girls of Kabul. A lot of people sleeping their way up. If you're with a small NGO with no money, no one cares about you. If you're with the World Bank, suddenly everyone at parties wants to go home with you."

"You caught us at a funny time," Lisa said to me by way of explanation. "We're all about to leave. I've got two months left. Nick's got four. Simona's leaving next month. We're all just looking not to take risks anymore, not to take our chances but survive instead and get out of here alive."

Nick was talking about things he meant to do in Afghanistan, places he meant to visit, which he probably never would. He still had a few months remaining, but his organization had asked him not to travel. They wanted to stay in their house, behind the walls, behind the guards, and just not die. They wanted what my hotel was selling, the sense of security, the sense of wearing an armor.

Lisa filled out the application for a new job just before she came down to the party. "What's the job?" Nick asked, laughing maniacally. "Combing someone's ass hair?"

"Basically," she shrugged. The job was in Washington for an arm of USAID.

Simona said she enjoyed Afghanistan's leading export, hash. Janhavi said she longed for some good hash to help her through all this tension and anxiety, living essentially under house arrest, listening to endless news of maiming and killing. But calling a dealer was risky. By definition, a drug dealer was not someone she could trust, and there was no telling whom he might associate with. She fretted over this dilemma. Others were less scrupulous. Between the hashish-buying and the hostage-ransoming, the NGOs and the Western governments who funded them seemed to pay all of the Taliban's expenses.

For now, this party remained fueled solely by alcohol. Nick had put on his iPod, and we were singing and strumming air guitars between conversations. In truth we were all getting a little tipsy, and a little rowdy, more than was prudent. "Psycho Killer" by Talking Heads came on the stereo and brought the party to its climax. Everyone sang along:

> *I can't seem to face up to the facts*
> *I'm tense and nervous and I can't relax*
> *I can't sleep 'cause my bed's on fire*
> *Don't touch me I'm a real live wire*
> *Psycho Killer*
> *Qu'est-ce que c'est*
> *Fa-fa-fa-fa-fa-fa-fa-fa-fa-far better*
> *Run run run run run run run away*

It was a fitting theme song for Kabul.

The next day Janhavi told me via text that we really were too noisy the previous night, that her security guard had expressed concern to her employer, and she had gotten an earful about it. The cardinal rule for the expat living in Afghanistan was to keep a low profile in every way. Any behavior that drew any kind of attention was a security risk. In America, a noise complaint from the neighbors might bring the police. In Kabul, it might bring the Taliban.

Retrospectively I supposed I ought to have feared for my life the previous night. Thinking back, I knew that I should have feared the dark and silent neighborhood that I peered out upon from their back porch, should have feared its vague touch of menace, should have feared what nefarious forces lurked in it. But at the time, the little music we had playing stealing through the windows and out into the night and our discordant singalong felt like the only things challenging that silent and deathly darkness. The only things that felt like life. It was a good enough reason to forget to be afraid.

*****

After mostly getting over my hangover, I finally made it to the Kabul Museum. The majority of its holdings were destroyed during the civil war and then by the Taliban, humorless men coming into the building with sledgehammers smashing up anything non-Islamic. Still there remained Buddha statues that looked like Greek gods with the high nose bridges and the draperies that clung to the figures as though wet. Relief figures on the sides of urns looked like satyrs. And in one wing stood striking wooden pagan ancestor figures from Nuristan, "the land of light," which up until Islamization in the late nineteenth century was still called Kafiristan, "the land of infidels."

An American worked at the museum. Lisa had said that he was a friend, so I asked for him by name and went by his office. The dome of his head was entirely bald and reflected the dim museum lighting. A thick pair of black glasses framed his weary eyes. Indeed, he looked like the stereotype of an egghead professor.

He was irritated to see me, to be dragooned into entertaining a casual visitor. I dropped Lisa's name, but it made no difference. I asked him his area of specialty. "Mesopotamia," he said with a wry and melancholy grin, telling without telling the bumpy career that might have led him here. Mesopotamia was today's Iraq, not Afghanistan. I left him alone and wandered through the sad hallways by myself.

Directly across from the museum was a kind of bridge between past and present: the Darul Aman Palace, that European-style creation of the naively modernizing king Amanullah, felt like a misplaced building of Versailles. It had shared the fate of this country and was burned and bombed during the wars.

Amanullah, silly man that he was, went to Europe with his stylish queen Soraya to hobnob with European royalty for months, allowing her to appear in newspapers in a shoulderless (gasp!) gown. Naturally the conservatives managed a coup and reversed all his reforms.

During the civil war, the Taliban operated out of the palace, attracting the heavy shelling that left it the way it was now, broken down and haunted by history's ghosts. A short distance away, atop a hill, the Tajbeg Palace, equally Western and equally ruined, looked down over Kabul like our celluloid image of Dracula's castle.

*****

As I was getting ready to move onto Herat, news came that a car bomb went off a half hour earlier some distance across town from me. A "VBIED," in military parlance — vehicle-borne improvised explosive device.

I tried to picture where it had happened. Wasn't I there earlier in the day? When the dust cleared, three NATO contractors had been killed along with nine Afghans. And here I had stumbled right past the bomb like some kind of Mr. Magoo or the man who knew too little.

So it goes.

*****

Compared to Kabul, Herat was a city peaceful and prosperous. The sparkling new Herat airport, paid for by Western aid, was barely guarded. Actual working traffic lights existed at (I counted) two whole separate intersections within the city, a sight so marvelous in this country as to make one doubt one's senses. But of course everyone ignored those lights, useless marvels. Hotels still had guards with assault rifles peeking out from behind multiple steel doors, but they wore the expression of routine and even good cheer. It was a far cry from the haunted look the Kabulians wore on their faces like they could already smell the putrefaction of death on each other, on themselves.

Historically Herat was largely autonomous, almost independent of Kabul. It still was. Ismail Khan, the mujahedeen leader turned warlord turned self-proclaimed "Emir of Herat" turned provincial governor and minister in Karzai's government, still dominated Herat and did as he pleased, despite Karzai's best efforts to sideline him.

Indeed, the centrifugal nature of the constituent parts of Afghanistan, which ensured the weakness of the central government, was in many respects the country's defining characteristic, its greatest curse and its greatest strength. Americans have this idea, courtesy of *Rambo II*, that Afghans join together to fight off invaders when attacked. But in fact, the country fragments into a thousand pieces when invaded so as to become ungovernable. The foreign-imposed government finds collaborators at every corner as well as enemies, until it can no longer tell the difference between the two.

Herat was closer to Iran than to most of the rest of Afghanistan, and not only geographically but economically and psychologically as well. The violence of Kabul and Kandahar seemed a world away, barely relevant to the Heratians. Business with Iran was what mattered, bringing the city exceptional economic growth. Moneychangers displayed U.S. dollars alongside Iranian rials in their glass cases showing Supreme Leader Khomeini's stern visage.

Advice that came my way said that violence nonetheless brewed not so deep beneath the surface, and kidnappings still took place regularly. But even surface tranquility in this country felt like such a blessing that one felt churlish expecting anything more.

Part of Herat's independence was born of having been actually in charge. After Timur's death, his son Shah Rukh moved the capital of the Timurid Empire here, leaving his son Ulugbek to rule Samarkand as viceroy. Whereas Timur would have started a war with China but for his death, Shah Rukh normalized relations with Ming China under the Yongle Emperor, the builder of the Forbidden City, the man who sent the Eunuch Admiral to sail around the world. China liked to pretend to deal with foreign countries as though they were vassals but in practice recognized the necessity of treating at least powerful states as equals, and the Timurid Empire was a case study in the unavoidability of diplomacy.

The architecture of Herat showed this proud history. Stepping, shoeless, onto the gleaming marble grounds of Herat's eight-hundred-year-old Friday Mosque, I felt as though suddenly returned to Samarkand, to the glory of the Timurid renaissance. The Timurids had put the familiar blue tiles on the walls, beautiful in their circular motifs and floral patterns. Their predecessors the Ghorid rulers had built the original mosque to be much plainer. The white marble floor stretched grandly across the entire open courtyard. Walking across it felt like a fitting way to approach God. In the *iwan* or vaulted hall, white like a bleached shalwar kameez, two dozen or so men slept snoring out of the lazy early afternoon sun. Men prayed in the corners, standing facing Mecca or kneeling devoutly. I, the atheist, slipped past them as quietly as I could.

I circled westward to the Herat citadel. The imposing fortress traced all the way back to Alexander the Great in 330 B.C. and was still known in Pashto as "Sikander Kala," or Alexander Fortress. But the present structure was largely the work of Shah Rukh, in 1415. Fragments of sapphire and turquoise Timurid tiling with

Kufic Arabic script still hung on the so-called "Timurid Tower" on the northwest.

Renovations as recent as 2011, partially funded by Washington, however, had left the citadel with an air of even more recent vintage. The place didn't quite have a new car smell. But it was difficult to visualize the bitter defenders within and the fierce invaders without when the Qajar Dynasty of Persia laid siege to this city in 1837-38, and these walls were all that stood in the would-be conquerors' way.

I exited the citadel and turned down a small alley. There I passed by a man standing just outside his door and his high walls (an Islamic custom to protect the modesty of the women within). He did a double take upon seeing me. What is this? A foreigner? When he recovered his composure, he gestured for me to come into his home.

For a moment, I stood there frozen, hesitant. I wanted to accept. Desperately. How wonderful it would be to be invited into a random Afghan's house, to share a meal with him, to experience the kindness of a stranger so far removed from our everyday experience as to seem alien. How exciting it would be to cross that threshold to embrace the unknown. And the first thing I did upon entering Afghanistan was to sit down with those border officers for lunch. Now that I had reached my last stop in Afghanistan, how nice would it be to complete the circle.

And yet...

The "and yets" and the "what ifs" got the better of me. A stranger off the street could be a Taliban collaborator or one of the entrepreneurial kidnappers—couldn't he? I waved at him, apologetically. Then I moved on, dragging behind me the weight of regret.

In the northwestern quarter of the city, I found the Timurids' last great architectural legacy in Herat, even in its utterly tragic and dilapidated state. Shah Rukh's wife, Ulugbek's mother, Gawhar Shad, built the Musalla Complex, possibly the zenith of Islamic architecture not only in Afghanistan but anywhere in the world. Almost all of that achievement had been destroyed. Just enough remained to allow the visitor to imagine the splendor that must have been and to leave him with the deepest regret of what no longer was. Most of the damage occurred in 1885, when British engineers dynamited the place to give army artillery a clear line of sight against an expected Russian assault, which of course never came.

On the north side, four colossal minarets still stood, looking like giants that Don Quixote would charge against. They were the survivors of a much more numerous original cohort, and they marked the corners of the destroyed Baiqara madrasa.

On the right, between the northeastern and southeastern minarets, a lone man in white slept in a hovel amidst some white flowers that had grown up, careless of the mid-morning sun that shone ruthlessly upon him.

Before him, between the road and the ruins, a little creek flowed but only barely. Filled with trash and sickly green algae, it was less of a creek now and more of a sewer. Along the road, vendors had racks of sunglasses set up. Motorcycles rode by, the vibrations of the traffic gradually undermining the foundations of even these surviving towers.

Behind the sleeping man, amidst the ruins where some doorways of the original structure were still extant, men scurried in and out, squatting in them as though they were caves. More men lay sleeping on the other side of the road, under the long shadows of the other two minarets. One man in filthy, tattered rags accosted me. I got away from him.

Beside the northwestern tower, an indentation in the ground now served as a garbage dump. Between these two minarets, the bottom halves of the structures still remained along with an elegant tombstone in a protective cage, and children played in the ruins. Taken together, the four minarets exuded a funereal grandeur, a dystopian majesty, as witnesses to lost glory, who stood stoic and tall and proud even in the face of such filth and indignity.

I moved south into the enclosed park that formed the rest of the complex. A single minaret from Gawhar Shad's madrasa remained, leaning toward the grimy road outside the complex as determinedly as the Tower of Pisa. On one side of it some of the blue tiling still remained, floral patterns that even as fragments showed tremendous beauty. Similarly, through a recently planted little forest, a single minaret of the original mosque survived, or rather half a minaret: a Russian RPG had cut it down by the waist during the war. Even the small proportion of the tiling that remained showed an intricate and original design.

Robert Byron in *The Road to Oxiana* rhapsodized about these minarets and what they represented. He would have seen the mosque minaret before the Russians took the top off. This was what he saw:

> ... no photograph, nor any description, can convey their color of grape-blue with an azure bloom, or the intricate convolutions that make it so deep and luminous. On the bases, whose eight sides are supported by white marble panels carved with a baroque Kufic, yellow, white, olive green and rusty red mingle with the two blues in a maze of flowers, arabesques and texts as fine as the pattern on a tea-cup. The shafts above are covered with small diamond-shaped lozenges filled with flowers, but still mainly grape blue. Each of these is bordered with white faience in relief, so that the upper part of each minaret seems to be wrapped in a

glittering net.

Noting that "minarets are generally the least elaborate parts of a building," Byron added, "if the mosaic on the rest of the Musalla surpassed or even equaled what survives today, there was never such a mosque before or since."

And now even the remnant minaret that he saw had been cut down by Russian firepower. As a symbol of vengeance, a burned-out Russian tank, mangled and rusted, lay next to the broken column.

Finally, there was Gawhar Shad's own mausoleum. Sarcophagi lay silent at the center of the building, and carvings like clamshells decorated the ceiling. Curiously they had turned the building into a haphazard library: bookshelves on all sides held volumes in Farsi and English, such incongruous items as the *Norton Anthology of Poetry* and a 2002 Windows XP manual oddly keeping each other company.

A lone librarian stood behind a table, messaging friends on Facebook. Seeing me come in and flustered by the unexpected appearance of a foreigner, he offered me tea. His name was Qodsi, and he didn't speak much English. Unfortunately, my Dari was still limited to the numbers one through one hundred, hello, goodbye, thank you, please, excuse me, and so on. So we communicated mostly through waving our arms around and drawing pictures in his notebook.

It turned out we were the same age. He asked me if I had a wife. I said no and asked him if he did. He said, "she gone." I surmised from his downcast look that she had died, and I was sorry that I asked.

"Afghanistan, not good," he said, without indicating whether this observation had anything to do with his wife's passing.

"Herat is okay," I said.

"Herat okay, Herat Persian people, okay. Pashtuns, ta-ta-ta-

ta," he imitated the noise of gunshots then made the same throat-cutting gesture that my weird Tajik lunch-buddy in Samarkand had made, only in a very different context. He was trying to warn me. "Afghanistan, Pashtuns, not safe, yeah? Not safe."

"Right," I answered, "it's not safe here. I know."

"Not safe foreigner. Go, go, go."

"I'll go to Iran soon," I offered.

"Iran?" He looked at me inquisitively as though wishing to make sure that he understood correctly.

"Me," I pointed at myself then turned that finger to some vague point in the distance. "Iran."

"Ah, okay, okay." Qodsi was glad to hear that I would get out soon.

Qodsi showed me to a shack by the park entrance. An elderly man missing half his teeth sat there selling glassware. The old man offered me tea as well with great solicitude. I sat with him and drank from his dirty glass. Surprisingly he spoke some English, but it was hard to understand through the gaps in his teeth.

The old man's face was as craggy as the Hindu Kush, and his beard draped over it like the snow. He was gaunt under his grimy blue robe. A length of blue cloth was tied around his left palm, bandage for a wound. Above it, on his wrist, was a crude tattoo of the name of Allah. I thought he looked like a statue symbolizing the battered spirit of his nation. He took me to the mud kiln at the end of the park and showed me how he fired the glass.

Just when Qodsi was despairing of further communications with me, another man arrived on a motorcycle, young and urbane looking. Qodsi jumped up excitedly. "English! English!" he cried. Hamayoun turned out to be the local museum director and indeed spoke fluent English. The educated man of the lot, he offered to show me old maps and photos of the Musalla and Herat, so we returned to the library.

Hamayoun took out his laptop and began showing old photos from the Niedermayer-Hentig Expedition of 1915-16, when the Central Powers in World War I sought to rally Afghanistan to their side. These were lovely images of the citadel in better conditions and the Musalla with several more minarets still standing, as well as sensitive portraits of Afghans in their daily lives. But as I admired them, Hamayoun got suddenly exasperated.

"Look at them!" he cried. "They look exactly the same as they do today. No change. No difference. No advancement. A hundred years, and we're still the same." It was true that the photos could've been taken yesterday.

He pointed an accusatory finger at the old man with a white beard in one black and white photo.

"These people had no plan," he said, "and we have no plan today." By "plan" he meant vision for the future, long-term strategy.

And his job depended on plans, restoration plans and conservation plans. There weren't any, he told me, because the government was entirely preoccupied with security problems.

"Everyone just thinks about today," he said. "Where to find food. Security. Nothing about education for our children. No plan for the future. We always just wait for foreign people to come help us. Americans, British, Chinese. We have no plans ourselves."

I had to agree with him wholeheartedly on the value of self-reliance.

The next photo was one of King Habibullah with his son the future King Amanullah, in Western military uniforms. "He had a plan," Hamayoun pointed at Amanullah, the failed modernizer and deposed monarch. "And they kicked him out because of it."

Hamayoun had experiences with the would-be saviors of Afghanistan. After the faded pictures of Niedermayer and the more recent ones by Professor Bruno of Italy, who came to study Timurid architecture in the 1970s, Hamayoun showed me photos of himself posing before landmarks in Berlin and Washington, D.C.

There he was, beaming in front of Capitol Hill. And there he was outside the White House, looking as pleased as a college boy in Cancun.

The next photo was of a shirtless blond man, definitely not Hamayoun, with one fist raised high in protest just outside the White House fence.

"A friend of yours?" I asked.

"This man," Hamayoun pointed to him, "was standing right outside the White House, and he was shouting, 'Fuck Obama, fuck Obama.'" He shook his head and licked his lips in deep appreciation. "That's democracy, man."

But when the foreigners did come trying to help, the help was ineffective.

"Say a European organization sets aside two million dollars for a restoration project," he explained. "A lot of that money goes to plane tickets for their experts to fly over and take pictures. A lot goes to drivers and whatever. At the end of the day, how much of the two million is really spent on restoration? Two hundred and fifty thousand?"

To me he was echoing Janhavi's words from a different perspective.

I whiled away much of the afternoon at the Musalla. Finally, it was time for me to go. Indeed, it was just about time that I left for Iran. Qodsi, who had sat to one side in awkward incomprehension while Hamayoun and I talked, now realized suddenly that I was leaving. He jumped out of his seat.

"I love you," he cried as I walked out the door.

Hamayoun laughed. "He does not understand that it is quite strong to say I love you," he said.

I turned to face the forlorn widower. "I love you, too," I said.

And I loved Afghanistan.

6

TWELVE ANGRY MULLAHS

VILLAGES OF MUD brick houses stood before the farthest western extension of the Hindu Kush, spread along the outskirts of Herat on the road to Iran. Their streets were the desert plain. Shepherds led their flocks through them. Dark silhouettes of covered women went about their day. Bales of hay lay on the opposite side of the road. But for the power lines, I would have thought that I had tumbled into a time machine and returned to the age of Timur or Ahmad Shah Durrani, the founding king of Afghanistan as a nation.

Then as the mountain range came to an end, the land opened up into a plain that stretched seemingly infinitely to the horizon. This was Khorasan, the ancient region that cut across modern borders to include both Afghanistan and much of eastern Iran.

I had made a posse with three Afghans, friendly men who offered me their snacks. A couple of hours after passing by these settlements west of Herat, we pulled up to the Afghan side of the border. It was bustling like a Sunday market, nothing like the Afghan-Uzbek border in the north where I walked alone across the Friendship Bridge. Trucks German, Polish, Russian, Chinese, and Taiwanese jostled against each other to pass. Our car threaded through them like a needle in the hands of a seamstress.

The four of us got out and went inside the border control office. My Afghan companions got their passports stamped after a modicum of elbowing others out of the way. But I faced an apparent official who displayed more interest in me than I might have liked. I say apparent official because he was wearing a plain white shirt and jeans. The only object on him that denoted authority status was a walkie-talkie strapped to his belt.

"Please," he said to me with the slightest undertone of a threat, "sit." Then, unprompted, he added, "I am very important here." Was he trying to impress me? "I am like FBI." I supposed that if they let him dress like this, he must've been important.

"Are you married?" He followed up.

"No."

"But I think you have girlfriend."

"Maybe."

"Yes, because you don't come to find Afghan women."

Surely not. That would be scandalous. I allowed myself a sheepish laugh. "No, no..."

He pointed to the uniformed man sitting next to him. "This guy, he's good police officer. But he has no girlfriend. He wants girlfriend. No girlfriend." The poor guy blushed and stared at a dusty corner. I felt bad for him. His superior was bullying him to show what a big man he was. For my benefit. To impress the foreigner.

The "FBI" man took his time with the rare New Zealander while my Afghan companions waited anxiously outside. Finally, he let me go, and my companions and I proceeded across the barely demarcated border to the Iranian side.

The Iranian passport control hall presented an entirely different scene. It made me miss the FBI man desperately. "Two minutes," said Sadr, the driver, pointing at the building, with what in retrospect was incredible optimism.

"Two minutes?" One of my companions, a bespectacled man with gentle manners, interjected. "Two hundred minutes," he said with a bitter laugh. He was much closer to the mark.

We took all our bags and got in line. Portraits of the Ayatollah Khomeini and his friendlier-looking successor the Ayatollah Khamenei looked down from a banner hanging from the other end of the hall, some twenty meters ahead.

A very long twenty meters. The line of men — only men, as their womenfolk sat in the aluminum seats and waited — crowded into each other, standing too close for my taste in the early afternoon heat, afraid to lose their places, even though the line was hardly moving at all. So it was that we waited in a miasma of male body odors and some sickly efforts at disguising said odors. Once in a while someone would push a trolley laden with boxes of fruits or rice up to the line and demand passage, and we would squeeze sideways, almost tripping over our own belongings.

And then the lone immigration officer servicing this line got up and stepped out from his booth. Lunch. He didn't return for an hour, and no one replaced him. No one even said anything about when he might be back. The formerly slowly crawling line came to a complete halt, like a centipede that dropped dead. For a full hour we stood in line waiting for nothing at all.

*****

Bored in line, I opened my copy of *The Decline and Fall of the Roman Empire*. Appropriately, I was on the chapter where Gibbon digressed to account for the rise of Islam. Having expounded on the life and career of Mohammed, Gibbon turned to the Arab-Muslim invasion of Persia, the battle of Qadisiya that broke Persia's back, the escape of Shah Yazdegard III, and the battle of Ecbatana that finished off Persian power, what the Arabs called "the victory of victories." Yazdegard fled east beyond the Oxus and

> ... solicited, by a suppliant embassy, the more solid
> and powerful friendship of the emperor of China. The
> virtuous Taitsong [Taizong], the first of the dynasty of
> Tang [a mistake by Gibbon — Taizong was the second
> emperor of the Tang] may be justly compared with the
> Antonines of Rome: his people enjoyed the blessings
> of prosperity and peace; and his dominion was
> acknowledged by forty-four hordes of the Barbarians
> of Tartary. His last garrisons of Cashgar [Kashgar] and
> Khoten [Khotan] maintained a frequent intercourse
> with their neighbors of the Jaxartes and Oxus; a
> recent colony of Persians had introduced into China
> the astronomy of the Magi; and Taitsong might be
> alarmed by the rapid progress and dangerous vicinity
> of the Arabs. The influence, and perhaps the supplies,
> of China revived the hopes of Yazdegard and the zeal
> of the worshippers of fire; and he returned with an
> army of Turks to conquer the inheritance of his fathers.

But the hapless Yazdegard was betrayed and murdered before he ever had a chance to test his arms against the Arabs once more. The Caliphate confirmed its conquest of Persia without unsheathing a sword. Yazdegard's son Firuz, "an humble client of the Chinese emperor, accepted the station of captain of his guards." Yazdegard's grandson "inherited the regal name; but after a faint and fruitless enterprise, he returned to China, and ended his days in the palace of Sigan [Xian]."

*****

I had a professor in law school who liked to say, "There is no justice; there is only the equitable distribution of injustice." After practicing law for some years, I had to concur.

The story of Iran can be understood as such: a series of lawsuits that can only be tried in the court of history, that are ultimately irresolvable, where no justice is truly possible. But that impossibility only makes the complaints more bitter, not less, and the search for an equitable distribution of injustice all the more urgent.

Consider the 7th-century Islamic invasion as the first fundamental dispute. With it, classical Persia was lost forever. Without it, the Iran we know today, where the people were Muslims and the language was written in the Arabic alphabet, would not be possible. In the court of history, the spirit of Persia could complain that the invasion and the destruction of ancient Persian culture ought not to have happened. But could modern Iranians wish for its reversal? Then they wouldn't be who they were.

Shiite Muslims might bring the second lawsuit against the Sunnis, on account of over thirteen centuries of persecution. By now, although Iran is primarily Shiite, globally Sunnis outnumber Shiites ten to one. My first stop in Iran embodied this complaint.

Mashhad was Iran's holiest city. Ali al-Raza, or Reza, or Razavi, was the eighth Imam of Shiism, and by the reckoning of that denomination the rightful heir of the Prophet Mohammed. Mamoun, son of Haroun al-Rashid the Abbasid caliph, murdered Reza with poisoned grapes. That was in 818 A.D.

And it was neither the first nor the last time the Sunnis murdered the leader of the Shiites. There was Ali, struck with a poisoned sword while praying. There was Hussein watching the slaughter of his whole family on the battlefield before being cut down himself. And there was Reza's father Musa, killed by Haroun. No wonder the Twelfth Imam supposedly just disappeared to become the Hidden Imam and would return Christ-like on some indefinite future date.

But could Reza's dead soul demand in the court of history that all of these murders be reversed? If they were, then Shiism wouldn't be Shiism: the religion of grief.

I can say the same about many other things, both historical and personal. My father spent his life resenting the outcome of the Chinese Civil War in 1949, when he was less than one year old. But had it not gone down the way it did, he never would have lived the (pretty good, all things considered) life he did. Certainly he never would have met my mother and had the family that he had.

As for me, my life at this juncture by conventional standards had hit a serious snag. My legal career was most likely at an end. Little more of my relationship with Ashley now remained other than old photos on memory drives. The life I had spent a decade and half building in America was gone like a dream from the night before.

And yet, it was only with exile that I could undertake this unlikely journey and could write about it now. Without it, I most likely would never have found the resolve to leave a lucrative job that no longer satisfied me.

And, although I had no way of knowing—as I ambled down the dusty roads of Mashhad—what opportunities exile would open up for me, I knew for sure that they would not be possible without exile. Will I one day wish not to have had those opportunities? There was no telling, not until many years from now. By that time, I will have been so shaped by the experiences afforded me by this path that to wish not to have had them will be to wish to be another person entirely.

In any event: back to Mashhad.

Mamoun buried Reza in Mashhad with pretended piety, leaving Mashhad to become a place of pilgrimage for Shiites everywhere. Haram-i Razavi, the Shrine of Reza, dominated Iran's second largest city. Everything else seemed dedicated to serving this resting place of the martyr. Dozens of four- and five-star hotels, meant for the wealthier pilgrims and meretricious as though displaced from Dubai, lined the street leading up to the shrine and named after the interred. As many pedestrians crowded the sidewalks as anywhere in China. Outside the shrine, loudspeakers blared prayers and invocations.

Human waves of pilgrims, women all in black burqas, their husbands beside them, small children in tow, the elderly and disabled in wheelchairs, helped along by sons and daughters and nephews and nieces, all crowded onto the shrine grounds. The praying and the kneeling and the preaching and the overwhelming grief they felt recalling the death of a virtuous man twelve centuries ago—this was the spiritual ecstasy that was the hallmark of the Shiites.

Entering each courtyard, they kissed the thick wooden doors. And inside each courtyard I could barely find a spot to stand without being pushed aside or elbowed or bumped into or being told by one usher or another waving a green duster to move along.

Chandeliers hung from the ceilings in the lower-level chambers, with glittering pieces of glass on the columns and walls, so that the place had the effect of a glitzy variation on funhouse mirrors. I would later find other, even more spectacular examples of glasswork throughout Iran, like the tomb of Emir Ali in Shiraz.

*****

In view of lawsuit number one, *Ancient Persia v. Arab Invaders*, I left Mashhad in pursuit of one more lost city. Suyab in Kyrgyzstan had postdated Gan Ying's mission, and Marakanda or Samarkand he likely would have seen but was not mentioned in the *Hou Han Shu* by name. But Hecatompylos he definitely visited on his mission, or as definite as we can be about events that happened over nineteen centuries ago.

Alexander the Great made a stop in Hecatompylos in 330 B.C. After his death, the city became part of the Seleucid Empire. Then the Parthian Arsacids made it their capital when they took power in Persia. This was why Gan Ying came here, to visit King Pacorus II in his capacity as envoy of the Celestial Court. In 101 A.D., Pacorus sent his own ambassador to China, presumably to reciprocate Gan Ying's visit.

Hecatompylos would have been quite a city then. Its very name suggested its scale: the Greek word meant "one hundred gates," as opposed to the typical four gates of traditional walled cities. Though presumably a figure of speech meaning "many gates" instead of literally one hundred, the name gave an idea of what the ancient Parthian capital might have been. By now, of course, it was lost to history along with all of ancient Persia.

I began making my way across northeastern Iran toward Hecatompylos, one bus at a time, one town at a time.

First stop: Nishapur, once the capital of Khorasan, founded by the Sassanian king Shapur I in the 3rd century A.D. It became one of the four great cities of Khorasan along with Herat and Balkh in Afghanistan and Merv in today's Turkmenistan. The great poet Omar Khayyam was from here. But when the Mongols came in 1221, they killed every last inhabitant and left the corpses rotting in the sun. Local farmers still dig up their skeletons in the fields from time to time. You can say a lot about the Mongols, but you can't accuse them of not being thorough. The Nishapur I saw was a dusty provincial town with nothing to show for its 1,800-year history. Even the monument to Omar Khayyam was in fact a modernist piece built in the 1970s.

I moved on for Damghan, a town of some fifty thousand and one step closer to Hecatompylos. But the bus I caught on the wayside, I learned, would not actually get to Damghan. It supposedly reached the town just before it, Shahrud. On the outskirts of Shahrud I found out that this wasn't entirely true either when the bus driver told me to get off there and hitch a ride into town. I stood by the side of the road and stuck out one thumb.

But then another bus stopped, smaller and more local-looking. "Damghan?" I asked the driver. He waved me aboard. Inside, my foreignness caused a commotion.

The driver told me to sit in the front seat next to him. "Afghani?" he asked, much to my surprise. Did I look Afghan in any way, now that I had put away my Afghan clothes?

"*Chin*," I said, once again giving the easy, racially appropriate answer instead of saying New Zealand which would only confuse him.

"*Chin, Chin, Chin*," the driver, a gaunt man in late-middle age, repeated over and over, slapping one hand on his dashboard maniacally as he did so. I wanted to tell him to focus on the road. I also gathered from his hand gestures that the vehicle he drove was a Chinese import.

Behind us, the other passengers bellowed questions and jokes in Farsi, and the entire bus suddenly became a scene of lively comedy and laughter, with me at center stage. I wished I understood them. Of course, in the windy bus, with the engine running laboriously under my seat, even if my Farsi were much better, I would likely not have caught much of what they were saying. Two names cut through the din, though: "Jackie Chan" and "Bruce Lee."

Then one man with a receding hairline in the middle of the lot said, "lunch." I looked his way to see if he'd elaborate. "Home, lunch," he said gesturing for me to come toward him. I wasn't sure whether he was serious. I had also been looking forward to seeing something of the vaunted Persian hospitality. Now that I was out of Afghanistan, the desire to let my guard down and accept serendipitous invitations was strong.

"Okay," I said, "let's go." I still wasn't sure if he was serious.

But when the bus next stopped, which was only a few kilometers farther than when I first got on it, Mohammed got up and took my backpack with him. So he was serious. I followed him off the bus, leaving behind the chorus of hilarity.

Mohammed led me down a quiet and dusty street to a modest house behind a steel gate painted brown. A somewhat dented Peugeot was parked in the yard. He led me into his house and invited me to sit down on the carpet. A figurine of a cowboy stood on the shelves opposite along with other odds and ends.

Clearly for my benefit, he changed the channel on the television from Sponge Bob Square Pants dubbed in Farsi to an English-language (presumably satellite) channel with Farsi subtitles. An awful Hollywood rom com came on. Right as Mohammed landed on the channel, two characters began a fairly graphic conversation about sex. I desperately wanted to know what the Farsi subtitles might have read.

His son, a little boy perhaps six or seven, came out to greet his father. The two of them went inside, leaving me in the living room. Quiet conversations emanating from the back indicated the unseen presence of a woman, his wife.

When Mohammed returned with our lunch, he had taken off the shirt he was wearing, leaving the undershirt and showing himself to be stereotypically hirsute. I appreciated Mohammed's hospitality, but he spoke no more English than I spoke Farsi, a fact that left us eating in silence while dialogues about modern American dating played in the background. I had never regretted my inadequacy as a student of the Persian language as much as I did then. I tried my best saying a few words of Farsi. But my sallies into conversation met repulses of blank looks.

With the food eaten, I conveyed my gratitude before inquiring as to how I should reach Damghan. Mohammed seemed to indicate that he would drive me—this impressed me if he was actually going to do so, as Damghan was an hour away. He put on a fresh shirt. I put my luggage in the dented Peugeot in the front yard. For a moment, at the far end of the house, I spotted his wife in a hijab that looked more like a cut of curtain cloth. I waved at her, and she waved back from that distance. That was all I saw of the lady of the house.

Mohammed pulled out of the yard and began driving me through Shahrud. It dawned on me after a few minutes that he was showing me the town. He stopped at a park lined with pine trees and indicated that I should take a walk. I declined. He stopped at a water park where children played and indicated that I might wish to get out. I declined. He pulled up beside a shooting range—"ta-ta-ta-ta," he explained onomatopoetically while miming a submachine gun. I declined. He made the gesture of washing one's hair, which mystified me until we wound up outside a bathhouse. I declined.

I supposed that he was showing me what the residents of Shahrud considered their town's top attractions, and I must have come across as very difficult to please. Then we stopped at another park and took selfies. He took a half dozen on his phone, getting finicky about the light and the background. I figured he wanted evidence to show his friends that a foreigner really did hang out with him for an afternoon.

Finally, he left me by half a dozen taxis parked on the way to Damghan. So he wasn't going to take me himself after all. No matter. I reached my next stop before sundown.

The final stretch of this little treasure hunt occurred the following day. Hecatompylos was now called Shahr-e Qumis or simply Qumis or Sarddavazeh (Persian for "one hundred gates," same meaning as the Greek), and it barely appeared on the map. The nearby village that would have to serve as the landmark was called Qusheh. It would take some effort to find.

When I finally found the site of Hecatompylos, I found in it a particular sadness, a particular desolation, that exceeded what I found in Suyab or Marakanda. In Marakanda, the old city lay buried under a field of dirt, but a museum on one side marked the area for what it was and celebrated what had been unearthed and what they represented. In Suyab, local farmers pointed the way, and a lone metal sign confirmed the place.

Here in Hecatompylos, a capital of the once mighty Arsacid Empire though it was, simply no one cared. In the village of Qusheh, a scattering of mud brick houses on the southern side of the Tehran-Mashhad highway, nothing pointed to the ancient city. Only one local resident seemed to know anything about it and also only in the vaguest of terms. Instead of excavating the ancient city, the Iranian government had plans to build a theme park twenty miles away and call it "Hecatompylos." That would be the gravest insult.

Only a few barren hints of the historic Hecatompylos remained. A few mounds in the earth, one of which might have been a Tower of Silence, where Zoroastrians left their dead to be consumed by vultures. There were the last remnants of an archway that was part of the royal palace. The villagers now used it as a garbage dump. Rubber tires, an improvisation also by the villagers, helped to shore up some of these structures.

I caught sight of a purplish piece at my feet that looked like it might have been carved, a broken, eroded fragment of a relief. For a moment I wanted to pick it up and take it with me. But in the end, I left it where it lay. If it was a relic of Hecatompylos, then it belonged here on the wind-swept plains of Khorasan.

Across from these ruins, a restored and obviously much younger caravanserai seemed the usurping protagonist on this stage. The locals said Shah Abbas of the Safavid Dynasty built it. That would date the building to the late-16th or early-17th century. It too was strewn with garbage.

So this was the royal city of Pacorus. What splendors might the Chinese ambassador have seen that were now forever lost? I could only imagine. Pacorus might have held a dinner in the ambassador's honor, as he sought to cultivate relations with China. What magnificent feast might he have served? The original Shiraz wine, perhaps.

These were mere fantasies. But the landscape was still here. The southeastern bastions of the Alborz mountains would have guarded the city from the north like red giants that staggered out of the Caspian Sea. To the south, the plains stretched far away, and one could picture real estate developers from two thousand years ago raising funds to put up new houses and baths and theaters for an expanding city. No doubt they would've assured their investors that this was a can't-lose business proposition: just look at the size and power of Persia.

Perhaps one day the archeologists would do their job and look under the detritus. For now, the secret magnificence of Hecatompylos would have to remain underground.

As I had failed to convey to my driver my reason for wanting to be here, he was now clamoring to go. He was an old man, hair all white that juxtaposed dramatically against his tanned, leathery skin. But now he displayed the impatience of a teenager.

I wished to commune with the ghosts of Hecamtompylos. I wanted a moment of ceremony, and even the garbage-strewn ground felt as though it obligated such ritual. Was there not some incantation I could recite, some poetry that would be appropriate as prayer, something to conjure the dead? Nothing came to mind. Only my driver's barking filled my ears.

I got back into the car wearing a long face. The old man in turn gave me a dirty look, the aged brows somehow looking particularly harsh as he frowned. To him, this was all a big waste of time. He stepped on the gas pedal and headed for Semnan.

*****

But I've been talking about these towns on the way to Hecatompylos and now to Tehran as though they were no more than dusty way stations. In fact, Semnan and Damghan were historic caravan towns where Silk Road traders and, yes, an ambassador from China, would have rested their feet, found a *chaikhana* or teahouse, and purchased some feed and water for their horses or camels.

Today they were unassuming towns with an old mosque here and a covered bazaar there. But one's imagination ran wild conceiving of all who might have passed through them with trains laden with silk or spices or melons or gold or, for that matter, gifts from one sovereign to another, be it from the emperor of China to Pacorus II or Yazdegard III to Taizong of the Tang.

*****

With my ticket to Tehran in hand, I was coming around to lawsuit number three: *Islamic Republic of Iran v. United States of America.*

An old man with hair and mustache all white was seated next to me. He began speaking to me in English. Like everyone before him, he asked me where I was from, and again for simplicity's sake I said I was from China.

"Mao Zedong!" he said upon hearing this. "You remember Mao Zedong?"

"I... I know who he was," I said. "But he had died by the time I was born."

"You like Mao Zedong?"

"Not really."

"Why not? He was a great man. Before him, Britain, other powers went to China, colonized. After him, China good."

"Well..." I frowned.

"Why don't you like him?"

"Have you heard of Chiang Kai-shek?"

"Chiang Kai-shek, Chiang Kai-shek... He was the leader of Taiwan, yes?"

"That's right, and he fought Mao. And, so, the truth is I'm from Taiwan."

"Ah, Taiwan."

"And there was another guy before the both of them, Sun Yat-sen..."

"Okay, okay, you know your history," he said with that lack of interest in learning anything new that many men above a certain age have. "I wouldn't know all of that. China and Iran both have long histories."

"That's true," I said.

"Egypt, Iran, and China, long histories." I thought he left out a couple of countries but held my tongue. "You know any Iranian history?"

"Well, I know about Imam Khomeini." Ayatollah Khomeini was posthumously granted the title of "imam," which technically he couldn't really be, as there could be no more imams of Shiism after the Twelfth or Hidden Imam, the Mahdi or Valiasr. My new friend laughed at this shallowness of understanding on my part.

"And Mosaddegh," I added to confound his expectations.

In the court of history, Prime Minister Mohammed Mosaddegh would surely be a star witness for Iran. Imagine the attorney for the plaintiff soliciting his testimony on the stand:

"Isn't it true," says the attorney, "that you were elected as the prime minister of Iran in 1951?"

Mosaddegh: "That's correct."

Attorney: "And just to be clear now, Prime Minister, was your election democratic? Was it free and fair?"

Mosaddegh: "Yes, it was."

Attorney: "It would be fair to say, then, that you represented the democratic will of the Iranian people?"

Mosaddegh: "That's correct."

Attorney: "Let us fast forward two years to 1953. Tell us, Prime Minister, what happened in 1953."

Mosaddegh: "You're referring to…"

Attorney: "Yes, I am."

Mosaddegh sighs mournfully with the pain of that memory written on his face. "In 1953," he says, "a coup d'état was launched against my government…"

Attorney: "And to your knowledge, who was behind that coup?"

Mosaddegh: "The American CIA, and the British intelligence agency, MI6."

"Objection!" cries the attorney for the defendant, the United States of America. "Hearsay!"

Attorney for the plaintiff: "We would like to submit into evidence Exhibit A, plans for 'Operation Ajax,' from the archives of the Central Intelligence Agency."

Attorney for the defendant mumbles something incoherent and fiddles with papers.

Back in reality, on my bus speeding toward Tehran, the old man's eyes widened. "You know about Mosaddegh? A great man, a great man."

"I'm sure he was."

Operation Ajax ultimately backfired on the U.S. and its allies. The people's outrage at the coup against Mosaddegh eventually led to the rise of the Ayatollah Khomeini and the Iranian revolution of 1979.

"I was a university student in Tehran at the time of the Revolution," my new friend said. "I'm sixty-three now, I was twenty-five then. But I remember it like it was yesterday."

I did the math quickly in my head. The numbers didn't add up, but close enough.

"I was going to go to study in Italy," he added wistfully, "but couldn't because of what happened. In the end, I never left Iran."

"I'm sorry to hear it," I said.

But my saying sorry made him suddenly defensive. "To be clear," he said, "I love my country. I think its people are better than people in other countries."

"Hey, come on," I nudged him with one elbow but never spelled out my point. He laughed.

I wanted to hear more of his memories of the Revolution, but he excused himself, took out a copy of the Quran from his bag and began chanting the *suras* softly. This was the proper way to read the Quran, in Arabic, out loud, and as a kind of singsong resembling a Gregorian chant. Let the music of the poetry transport you, because religion is a form of literature. He interrupted himself once to apologize to me for being noisy. I said it was no problem.

When he finished, he put away the scripture and returned his attention to me.

"Do you believe in God?" he asked.

"Sure," I lied, not just because I was in Iran but also because of the pious way he was just chanting the Quran.

"I think you have to believe in God, because God is big power, no? Big strength." I chose not to debate theology with him.

"You studied at university?" he asked.

"I did."

"What did you study?"

"Politics."

"Ah, political science, me too. I think political science is, how do I say, a beautiful science. No?"

"Yes... well, I'm not sure I'd use the word 'beautiful.'"

"Did you study Machiavelli?"

"I did."

"Did you study Jean-Jacques Rousseau?"

"I did."

"Did you study Montesquieu?"

"I did."

"What was the name of his book? In Persian it's called," he said a phrase in Farsi.

"*The Spirit of the Laws*?"

"Yes, yes, that's the one. And did you study Mitterand?"

"Mitterand? The former president of France? No..."

"Tell me—I ask you because you studied political science. When Americans talk about human rights, do you think they mean it? Because I don't think they mean it."

"Maybe sometimes they mean it."

"Sometimes!" he laughed at my qualification. "And what about the way Iran is now talking with the big countries? With America, with England, with France, with Germany." He meant the nuclear agreement that the Obama Administration was at this time working very hard to strike with Iran.

"I think it's good to talk."

"I think we did well in the talks. I think it will be good for Iran."

"I'm sure you'd like to see the sanctions lifted."

"What about for America? What do you think?"

"It's better for everyone to talk."

"More peaceful," he nodded with a frown of concern. But in the next moment he added that he felt that Americans were bad people. "They were not originally from America. Originally the people there were, uh..."

"Indians?" I decided that the term "Native Americans" might not have made it into his vocabulary yet.

"Yes, yes, so they invaded and came in."

I understood his point to be that Americans were congenitally an invasive, colonizing people, a tendency born of their history.

Historian Frederick Jackson Turner postulated the "frontier hypothesis" of American history, arguing that the country was largely a function of its ever-expanding frontier. Expansion came unquestionably with imperialism. And the pessimist in me saw that the frontier was the inherently racist division between us and them, the Self and the Other. But at the same time the frontier was the place where different currents and different cultures met, where people who embraced differences could go. America had long been an energetic and innovative country also because of its frontier nature. Rightly or wrongly, the latter vision of America was the one that I'd chosen to believe in for all these years.

When we reached Tehran, the old man apologized for not inviting me over for dinner.

"I want to have a Taiwanese guest," he said, "but today I cannot. No time. I am sorry." He showed me the ropes of the Tehran metro. As passersby did double takes and stared at the foreigner, we shook hands on the platform and bade each other farewell.

*****

In Tehran, I went looking for the former U.S. Embassy. This was where Kermit Roosevelt, Teddy's grandson, planned and carried out Operation Ajax against Mosaddegh's government. The scene of the crime, as it were.

And it was the scene of a second crime. When the Iranian revolution happened, in 1979, a group of armed university students charged the U.S. embassy and occupied it for over a year, holding dozens of Americans hostage.

The state of the embassy building, now used by the Revolutionary Guard, was the result of that occupation. A seal of the United States, half chiseled away as though it appeared on the face of some ancient, ruined temple, marked the complex's front entrance. Anti-American murals decorated the southern walls. One showed the Statue of Liberty as a skeletal goddess of death.

Perhaps here the United States would like to countersue Iran. Perhaps here counsel for the United States would lay out all the ways in which the Islamic Republic has been an oppressive and menacing regime. And the U.S. wouldn't be entirely wrong. But the fact remains that all that subsequently transpired was the fruit of the poisonous tree of the 1953 CIA-sponsored coup.

*****

The ruined embassy now stood as a symbol of American folly. Elsewhere in the city, the opulent Golestan Palace stood equally for the folly of the Qajar shahs. Similarly the nearby national collection of jewels, once belonging to the royals and now held in the Central Bank. For gemstones had a lot more role to play in Iranian history than you might think. Nadir Shah, for example, took the famous Koh-i-Noor diamond from Mughal India only to have his grandson give it to Ahmad Shah Durrani, founder of Afghanistan. Now the British held it as one of their crown jewels.

Set in the shadow of the mountain, modern Tehran might have been beautiful, but the million vehicles spewing black smoke into the air gave the city a dystopian aspect instead. Tehran did not exist in Gan Ying's time. The first mention of the village that would become today's metropolis coughing its lungs out occurred in the eleventh century. And Tehran was the rare city helped by the Mongol invasion rather than hurt or entirely leveled by it. When the Mongols sacked the nearby city of Rey, of which Tehran was just a satellite, the survivors of the Mongol onslaught escaped to this small village until it grew to be an important city itself.

Gan Ying, then, was unlikely to have passed through here. But a general southward arc tracing roughly through this part of Iran would have made sense for him coming in from Afghanistan. Southeast of Tehran, south of Hecatompylos, the desert of Dasht-i Kavir spread out far and forbidding. North of Tehran lay the Alborz mountains and the Caspian Sea. Although some have suggested that the "ocean" that Gan Ying came upon was the Caspian, the Gulf would make much more sense. And turning south from around here, Gan Ying would head toward the Gulf but also pass through the ancient cities of Esfahan, Shiraz, and Persepolis. That, then, was the path I'd follow.

But before heading south, there was something I had to see.

In the Alborz once stood the "Castles of the Assassins." Indeed, this was where the word "assassin" originated. Twelfth-century devotees of the Ismaili sect, a branch of Shiism often considered heretical, lived in these mountain fortresses and reputedly went around killing their enemies. Hassan-i Sabbah, their leader, "the old man of the mountain," supposedly got them high on hashish and then showed them secret gardens with beautiful women in them, leading them to believe that killing and dying for him would land them in paradise. For that reason, they were called *hashishin*, or men of hashish, whence the English word "assassin," whence the Spanish word "*asesino*" for "killer." At least that was the story that Marco Polo told in his *Travels*, which might have originated in slander by Sabbah's enemies.

In the historic town of Qazvin, the base camp for seeing the castles, I met jolly Mohsen, looking like a more corpulent version of Kal Penn. He agreed to take me to the Alamut and Lamiasar Castles. Mohsen was quick to laugh, even in a conversation proceeding partly by the vigorous waving of arms, and I liked him for it.

I was still wearing my Afghan scarf. He pointed to it and made a gesture of tying it up into a turban. "Imam Khomeini!" he said with utmost delight.

From Khomeini he got onto Khamenei, and from Khamenei to former president Ahmadinejad.

"Ahmadinejad bad," he said. "Ahmadinejad war." This was when I learned the Farsi word for war — *jang*. "Rouhani good," he added, referring to the current president.

Then he made a gesture of linking hands, thankfully not taking both hands entirely off the steering wheel, to indicate diplomacy or friendship. "Bush bad, Bush *jang*. Obama... Obama okay." He gave the more-or-less, plane tipping its wings gesture with his right hand.

"If Iran and America became friends," I said verbally and otherwise, "then a lot more foreigners could visit the assassins' castles."

He laughed and shook his head sadly like I was being preposterous with the notion of US-Iranian friendship.

He asked me if I was Muslim. I said I wasn't. He smiled forgivingly as though saying that no one was perfect.

"Muslims," he sighed and then mimed the throwing of punches, leading the car to wobble. "Christians no, Muslims," again pantomime boxing to indicate combativeness. I wanted to say those were his hand gestures, not mine, but I kept my mouth shut.

Alamut or "the eagle's nest" was our first stop. It was famous enough that the entire valley in this stretch of the Alborz was named after it. The castle was a steep climb up the craggy mountain that once held off Mongols and now discouraged those of us who hadn't been for a run in a long while.

The castle stood atop a thick gray rock. And it had a leaning shape to it, as though the high winds had blown it back like long tresses on the head of a woman riding in a convertible. And the remnants of the castle held a hint of a volute in it, a swirl. In that it conformed with the corkscrew shape of the mountain. Unfortunate scaffoldings cloaked the structure as though it were a Manhattan hotel under renovation. But a climb to the top, leaving the scaffoldings behind, revealed the panorama of the mountaintops all around and the green village of Gazor Khan beneath.

An Iranian family, a father with his three daughters, happened to visit at the same time as me. They pressed their picnic food into my hands. For a moment, I instinctively declined but then immediately saw the hurt in the father's face—I was being rude—and quickly reversed myself. The sweetness of the watermelon was a pleasant companion to the clear air high in the clouds. When I came down the mountain, they happened to follow a few minutes behind me, and meeting Mohsen, they had a smiling talk with him. It looked to me like they were making him promise to keep me safe — or else.

A couple hours away by the winding mountain road Mohsen pulled over. It seemed like the middle of nowhere. It was the middle of nowhere. He pointed to a path through the grass along a ridge and said, "Lamiasar."

"Here? Really?"

He waved emphatically for me to get out and get walking. I did as he said and was not misled. A few hundred meters on, the ridge turned purplish maroon, and a colossal rock of the same painted color stood in my way. A northerly wind blew here, strong enough to knock me off my feet.

The footpath continued up the rock. Behind it, on the southern side, sheltered from the wind — leeward if this were a boat — the remnants of the castle shot out from the crags and outer walls from the sides of cliffs like stalagmites. Whoever built this structure meant business. From the forecastle, the mountain ridges below alternated green with grass and purple with rocks like veins of gemstones. The cultivated valleys between them, from this vantage point, were lozenges of emerald.

I climbed atop what was left of the main castle and was once again exposed to the wind. I realized that I was completely alone. Stylishly alone. There were no other visitors, no Iranian family offering me food. The nearest human being was Mohsen back in the car. I turned to look for the car and could only just make out the dot of it on the other side of a steep valley. Alternately grassy and slippery paths led downward from where I stood, cliff-ward, to the remains of watchtowers and fortifications. Away from the purple veins, the harsh folds in the earth made me think of the Scottish Highlands.

What might it have been like to stand up here back in the 12th century with the Ismaili assassins, the wind threatening to carry you off with the birds? There certainly seemed no room for secret gardens or for beautiful women to keep their clothes and rouge. But the quietude here, the panoramic perspective over the world beneath your feet, the sense of the extreme—it seemed that whoever lived up here, the assassins, today we would variously describe them with words like "badass" or "gangster." I wished to stand there forever.

But no, after a few hours I'd be bored. And then I'd probably want some hashish. Or a secret garden with beautiful women in it. Or both.

It rained when I returned to Qazvin. Thunderstorm.

*****

But the ride to Esfahan, across the country's central plains, reaffirmed my arid image of Iran. One imagined Roman legionnaires, lost soldiers of Crassus or Julian the Apostate, wandering through the rocky sands seemingly held together by the clumps of rough grass like birds' nests. A far cry from the fields of Tuscany or the olive groves of Greece. As thirst clung to their tongues, surely even the stoutest standard bearers would have cursed their generals for leading them to this desert of the vultures. The story goes that after they killed Crassus, the Persians poured molten gold down his throat as mockery for his greed.

On the road south to the Persian Gulf, Esfahan had always been one of the country's great cities, the heartland of old Persia. Iranians like to say that Esfahan contained half the world. In Arsacid times, it was a major provincial capital, and Gan Ying likely passed through here on his way to the sea. But it became the great cultural marvel it was now much later, during the Safavid dynasty starting in the late 16th century. King Abbas the Great, the man who built that caravanserai across from the ruins of Hecatompylos, relocated his capital from Qazvin in the mountainous north to Esfahan.

It was, in fact, one of the finest places in Iran. The heart of the city gave off a pleasant air like one big Persian garden. Compared to Tehran, it was literally a breath of fresh air. Naqsh-e Jahan, the main square of Esfahan, was the second largest public plaza of its kind in the world, behind only Tiananmen Square in Beijing. Its name, meaning "Map of the World," indicated the ambition of its design.

Rasul, "Russell in English," sidled up to me and introduced himself. He looked young, I thought late teens, then he told me he was twenty. He wore aviator glasses — which turned out to make sense as he was studying to become a pilot — a starched white shirt, and carried a briefcase in his hand. He said he wanted to practice his English. I let him.

He brought up Bruce Lee. I had just been thinking if I had one more conversation about Bruce Lee, I might lose it. But I managed.

"You know," he said, "Iranians really admire him."

"That so?" I replied. He failed to catch the weariness in my voice.

He offered that he was learning *Sanda*, Chinese freestyle boxing, besides learning to fly planes and besides working in the silversmith shop on the corner. He also said that as a teenager he was the provincial track and field champion. I believed him. He seemed like the earnest type.

"Oh, I know how to write some Chinese words," he said. "Want to see?"

"Sure."

He took out a piece of paper and, with some hesitation, drew the character for wood or tree.

"Very good, I'm impressed."

"But Chinese people not so good at growing bread," he said, stoking the stubbles on his own chin. "Iran people, Arab people, good at growing bread."

"Beard," I said. "You mean beard." I'd heard Iranians confuse bread, beard, and bird.

"Ah, okay, okay." He practiced the three words, miming putting something in his mouth, stroking his chin, and flapping his arms. "What religion are you?" he asked.

"Buddhist," I lied. Why did everyone have to ask about religion here?

"Ah, yes, yes, Buddhism," he nodded knowingly, as though terribly familiar with the Eightfold Path.

"Is the water clean?" I gestured at the fountain near our end of the square, where young boys had jumped in and were splashing water at each other and squealing with pleasure. When the wind blew, droplets of the water landed on our faces, and the smell of half a dozen horse carriages a la Central Park on the other side of the fountain reached us as well.

"Mm, no," he replied.

I wiped my face with my sleeve.

He led me through the famous bazaar off the north end of Naqsh-e Jahan. "Everything in here, made in China. We look at label, made in China. We have a song, 'made in China, made in China,'" he sang a couple of repetitive lines atonally. "How do Chinese people think of themselves?" he asked.

"They think they're terribly smart, but then they complain about themselves all the time. They're proud of their long history, like Iranians."

"What about Americans? How do they think about themselves?"

I gave a diplomatic answer about how they were well-meaning but might not be well-informed about the rest of the world.

"And what do you think of Americans?" I asked, thinking of the decades-old, seemingly irresolvable conflict between Iran and the United States, the lawsuit pending in my imaginary court of history.

"I think," he replied, "I don't judge until I see America for myself."

I liked him for being fair-minded. How many Americans, I wondered, would decline to comment on the Middle East on the grounds that they hadn't visited personally?

The bazaar was labyrinthine enough that even he lost his way and stopped a couple of times to ask for directions. Eventually we turned a corner and found a space opening up before us. There it was, the Jameh Mosque, one of Esfahan's star attractions. Rasul led me inside and began playing the tour guide. The tile patterns on the walls, he noted for me, spelled not only Allah and Mohammed, as in the madrasas of Samarkand, but also the name of Ali, the first Imam of Shiism. But he was rushing through everything. Indeed, he was nonplussed that I wanted to see this place at all.

"For us, it is normal," he said. This was simply where he and his neighbors came for Friday prayers.

"Yes, but for us it's not," I said. "You know I cannot see this in my home country." I had adopted certain stilted expressions to make sure people understood me, like "home country." But in this moment the expression saddened me, and the sadness caught me off guard. I wasn't sure which country I was referring to. For a second I fell silent.

Rasul didn't notice my sudden reticence and merely nodded sympathetically.

The call to prayer sounded mournfully from the minaret.

Rasul excused himself to join in the prayer.

I sat back and took in the pigeons taking off from the sandbox. Just then another voice spoke to me.

"Where are you from?" I looked to my right and found a trio of young Iranian women sitting beside me and all staring at me. I was attracting a fair bit of attention as the foreigner.

"Taiwan," I said, varying my answer.

"We are from Shiraz," the girl who spoke continued.

"What's your name?" I asked.

"Sabah," she replied.

"I'm going to Shiraz after here."

"Ah, you must let me give you some recommendations."

I took out the little Moleskine notebook I carried with me. She scribbled some notes in it.

As we were speaking more and more young women gathered around. The hijabs they wore were more colorful than what one often saw. Soon it was as though a field of flowers surrounded me.

"Are you all in the same group?" I asked, gesturing at the lot of them.

"Yes, we are all together," Sabah said. "We are medical students." Ah, I thought, that explained the fluent English. I complimented her on it. "Thank you," Sabah said. "You speak very good English as well."

"I lived in America for a number of years."

"That explains it," she exchanged a look with her friend next to her. "We overheard you talking, so we knew you speak English very well. My friend was saying how interesting it was. I said people in other countries study English too. But if you lived in America, that makes a lot of sense."

I happened to use a Farsi word.

"Do you speak Farsi?"

"No, but I'm trying to pick up a few words here and there," I said. After a pause, I added, "Also I'm relying on the little Arabic I know. It's interesting to me, the Arabic loan words in Farsi."

"That's because they attacked us." She shrugged with a slightly mournful air about the disastrous defeat fourteen centuries ago that also brought Islam.

Lawsuit number one, the Arab destruction of ancient Persia, had returned to haunt us.

The chaperone came over and broke up the party. She wore the full black chador, not the flowery hijabs sported by the girls she was looking after. Only a pale face showed, dowdy looking behind rail frame librarian glasses. A humorless woman, I gathered.

"Time to say *khoda hafez*," she said, using the Farsi phrase for goodbye. The dozen or so medical students obeyed only with despondency and wished me good luck.

*****

In truth the Jameh Mosque was a world of tranquility closed upon itself, but only now that I'd been left alone for the second time was I able to appreciate this. The building was an architectural marvel riddled with many nooks and crannies, like a grand dame with many secrets. The many parts of the whole were in fact crafted in different eras in Iranian history.

The Sultan Ujeito room, for example, was found behind a closed but not locked wooden door. Why was it there? No matter. The mihrab inside, denoting the direction of Mecca for the faithful, was an intricate wooden mesh formed by Quranic inscriptions intertwined with floral patterns. On the far side of the room, hidden behind another low wooden door, was the cold-sounding fifteenth-century Winter Hall. The lights were turned off when I went inside, and the alabaster skylights were insufficient to raise the space above a monastic dusk and the peace that came with it.

On the north side of the building, hidden behind the north *iwan* and its blue moldings overhead pressing down on me, and behind the forest of columns that formed the prayer hall, was another bit of serenity that I couldn't quite explain: the Taj al-Molk Dome, nine hundred years old and mathematically perfect. Maybe that was the explanation for my serene feeling, mathematical precision.

Back in the central courtyard, two men brought a bag of bird feed to the sandbox on one side of the fountain. A regiment of pigeons descended on it. And every time someone came too close, they lifted off in the same moment and circled the courtyard in formation like pilgrims around the Kaaba in Mecca before landing again where they left their food. I sat on the marble floor and watched them go, round and round.

On the south end of Naqsh-e Jahan was another magnificent mosque, the Masjid-e Shah, or Mosque of the King. I wandered through and found the same sense of peace. No single element stood out for me as being particularly striking, but the accumulation of a million pieces of painstaking artistry was instead what made the building what it was. Perhaps whence the peace. In the expansive southern *iwan*, a hallowed feeling hung in the air amidst the blue tiles. In the main sanctuary, hollowness between the inner and outer domes produced an echo like dominoes. A single clap at the center of it resounded a dozen times or more, a dozen hints at infinity.

But it turned out that the evening was when Esfahan truly came to life. When the warm summer night descended, families sat on the grass in Naqsh-e Jahan for picnics. Shops all around lit up in neon colors. Ice cream parlors along the main street became busy thoroughfares.

I took a stroll across the old Safavid bridges, arcades of arches, lit up with warm yellow lights and romantic like something out of the *Thousand and One Nights*. But the river they spanned, the Zayandeh, had run dry for long enough for patches of grass to grow atop the cracked riverbed like some kind of cake straight out of the oven. An Arab man, his ethnicity marked by the plain white *keffiyeh* that he wore over his head, stopped me on the Khaju bridge to chat. He told me he was Iraqi, from Baghdad. Half a dozen Iranians stopped to take pictures of us, so fascinated they were by the sight of a Chinese talking with an Arab.

*****

In connection again with lawsuit number one, the fall of Persia to Islam, I went looking for the remains of the Atashgah Zoroastrian fire temple. Zoroastrianism was the dominant religion of ancient Persia. Islam, brought by Arab conquerors, swept away the old faith, save for a few remnants.

The Atashgah stood in the western suburbs of Esfahan. Even from a distance it looked like just my sort of thing, crumbling mud bricks set atop a hill of rocks that might have been a set from Conan the Barbarian.

A black rock covered in yellow dust transitioned into worn out stairs leading up to the heart of the sanctuary. Grooves trailing down the hill might have been a drainage system. Recessed chambers in the walls must have once held treasures, mementoes of the god of the Zoroastrians, Ahura Mazda. The remains of stepped structure on the far side attested to the original ziggurat form, the emulation of the mountain that is the oldest and most natural shape for religious architecture, from which the Greeks would so marvelously diverge.

A reconstructed cylinder at the top of the structure marked what would have been the holy of holies, the flames that formed the object of worship: Zoroaster/Zarathustra taught his followers to pray to light as the manifestation of Ahura Mazda, and fire was the only light source that man could control.

From this vantage point atop the tower, the serrated shape of the Sofeh Mountains that loomed over Esfahan seemed an object of longing. And here at the ruined temple, I was once again entirely alone.

*****

What Zoroastrians remained in Iran mostly congregated in the area around the city of Yazd, which I moved on from Esfahan to see. It was the sort of ramshackle desert town that one might describe as charmingly decrepit. Ingenious medieval air conditioning contraptions called *badgir* dotted the skyline of the old city like a whole lot of church organs.

A pair of towers of silence stood on the outskirts of town like husband and wife. Perhaps one was in fact for male sky burials and the other for the female ones. Atop each stony hill, a circular wall enclosed a stone-paved area with a pit in the middle, where the dead were left for the vultures. Between the yellow earth and the yellow sun, it almost felt as though predatory wings batted behind one's ears.

The Jameh Mosque of Yazd showed me something distinct from all the other mosques I had seen. Twin minarets flanked the entrance, resembling a pair of candlesticks, blue as though scented with lavender. A grand arch with turquoise studs on it shaped like breasts opened up into a cavernous hall like a train station that formed the main sanctuary. Patterns of diamonds and stars of baby blue decorated the interior of the dome, their forms gentle as the stars that a first-grade teacher might stick on the homework of children. At the center was a swirl looking like a carousel or the blades of a fan. Bowtie patterns left uncolored in the walls of the side corridors completed the surprisingly child-like atmosphere of this house of Allah. Nearby the Amir Chaqmaq displayed a similar pair of lavender candlesticks atop a facade of arcade that seemed as Palladian as anything in Italy.

*****

But wait—I forgot about, well, let's call it lawsuit number zero: *Ancient Persia v. Alexander the Great.*

"Alexander the Great?" Leilah said with a sneer, almost spitting on the ground. "No, no. It's Alexander the Damned, Alexander the Accursed."

It was true that, in this part of the world, Alexander or "Iskander" played the role of the bogeyman. Parents still sometimes told their children to behave "or else Iskander will come and get you."

Leilah was perhaps a handful of years younger than I, with the clothes and makeup that bespoke a Western outlook but with the fashion sense that in the West might have made her something of a nerdy girl growing up. She taught English at a language institute, she explained, having earned a B.A. in English translation and an M.A. in English language teaching. She now hoped to qualify for a university position. But still a few curious usages peppered her otherwise fluent English— "symptom" instead of symbol, "agent" instead of representative, "disadvantage" instead of injury. And she mispronounced "tomb" as "tome"—a common error, I'd noticed.

She was showing me around Persepolis alongside a couple of young Poles and a Spaniard. Persepolis was the soul of ancient

Persia, never mind that its name was Greek: "the city of Perse," which is to say, "Parsa" or Persia. The entire Persian empire, if it did not quite spring from Persepolis, then it was at least metonymically symbolized by it. Like the Ile-de-France in Paris, the small germ of an island on the Seine from which all of France seemed to have sprung.

Darius the Great began building the city in 520 B.C., with successors like Xerxes I and II and Artaxerxes I, II, and III continuing the work for over a century and half. Then came Alexander of Macedonia. Gleefully, he set it on fire in 330 B.C. The majestic ruins that remained now at once encapsulated the empire's greatness and also (to my mind) its shortcomings.

In the court of history, though, the attorney for Alexander has a good point that the Persians went around subjugating other nations long before Alexander was ever born. Did Achaemenid Persia not repeatedly invade Greece? Salamis, Plataea, Marathon that gave the world the twenty-six-mile run, and Thermopylae with King Leonidas and the Three Hundred. All that Alexander did, so his attorney may argue, was to repay the Persians in full.

And to make his point, the attorney for Alexander can point at Persepolis itself. The entrance of the complex, the "Gate of All Nations," demonstrated the Achaemenid dynasty's ambition to subsume and rule over diverse peoples, seemingly without appreciation or even an inkling of the difficulties of domination over distant and distinct nations.

The Apadana Staircase, with its bas-reliefs so well-preserved one wondered whether they were newly restored, displayed the many nations paying tribute to the Shah of Shahs. The Parthians who would rule Persia as the Arsacids took their place near the center alongside the Saka or Scythians and the Azari or Azerbaijanis. Ironically relegated as the least important to the end of the relief, where the stone wall ran out of space, were the

Macedonians and the Arabs who would take turns toppling all that the Persians ever built.

Leilah, though, could see no evil portent in the iconography. "See how they're holding hands," she pointed to the representatives of the many nations each bringing the special produce of his native country. "It was a peaceful time when all lived together." No empire could rise to power without violence and oppression, but she seemed oblivious of the necessary sins of Persia, or at least she chose to elide over them. To her, ancient Persia was all kumbaya.

In my eyes, the architecture of Persepolis also displayed a confusion of values. The grand columns seemed indistinguishable from Greek columns until one's eyes reached the capitals at the top, which were eclectic and thus complicated and ornate arrangements including typically Greek Ionic volutes as well as elements not reminiscent of the Greek. The capitals took up as much as a third of the lengths of the columns; they were excessive and the opposite of classical Hellenic simplicity even as they also displayed the same techniques found in Athens and Olympia, protesting their precedence and pedagogical status relative to the upstart Hellenes.

It was as though in their desire to include, the Persians failed to make up their minds about what they really wanted to represent, what they really believed. The same iconography used throughout the complex, such as the griffin, later an emblem for Christ, could stand for both good and evil. In one scene it was on the side of the shah, symbolizing his strength, and in the next the shah stabbed the griffin in the underbelly, a representation of the shah slaying his own hubris. And Persian hubris was the original hubris, so much so that Persia seemed the doomed hero of the Greek tragedy that was the *Histories* of Herodotus.

The double iconography seemed a premonition of the

dangerous philosophy of Manichaeism to come, the intertwining of darkness and light, the admixture of Ahura Mazda and Ahriman.

Leilah was also still upset about lawsuit number one, the Arab invasion in the seventh century. "Fucking Arabs," she said grinding her teeth. "Those barbarians ruined everything, all our culture and our country."

The way she talked about the Arabs seemed to embody the paradox of Islamic Iran. But for the Arab invasion, Iranians would all still be Zoroastrians. Yet the religion introduced by that cataclysmic, traumatic event was by now so intertwined with Iranian identity that it was surely inoperable. No justice was possible fourteen centuries after the fact; one could only strive for the equitable distribution of injustice.

How could one reconcile Islam and the invasion? Leilah tried heroically.

"Muslims are supposed to value knowledge and learning, you know," she pointed out. As the hadith said: "Seek knowledge; even as far as China." But the Arab invaders, she said, burned the records of the Sassanian Dynasty, leaving Iranians in the dark about their own early history. "That's why I don't feel they were really Muslims," she concluded.

But her reasoning here was tortuous. The invasion of Persia happened in the years immediately after the death of the Prophet Mohammed, so that the Arab-Muslim generals were "Companions of the Prophet," men who personally knew him. Khalid bin Walid, nicknamed "the Sword of God," first attacked Mesopotamia, today's Iraq but at the time Persian territory, only a year after the Prophet's passing. If these men were not true Muslims, one would be hard-pressed to name any true Muslim in the history of the world.

Leilah's views of history, though, explained her politics.

"There are two kinds of leaders in our government," she told me. "There are those who want to be like Arabs, and there are those who want to return to an older Persia." In her formulation, the former group was made up of the dour mullahs and the religious hardliners, while the latter included the moderates and modernizers. The age-old feuds, what I've been calling lawsuits of history, shaped Iranian politics even today.

Old Persia, in her view, was not so different from the modern West. "You should see how Iranians party behind closed doors," she said. "It's just like a Western party," She painted a Gatsby-esque picture of Tehran nightlife with the bright young things. "Swimming pools filled with liquor, why not." I promised her that most parties in the West were not like that.

While on the subject of alcohol, one of the Poles and I lamented our inability to drink Shiraz wine in Shiraz, given Iran's official alcohol ban.

"Oh, no problem," Leilah said nonchalantly. "My cousins make their own wine at home from Shiraz grapes. At their house in the country. You want to go?"

"Uh…" The Europeans and I hesitated. Maybe fashionable young Iranians got away with debauchery. But foreigners drew attention and risked much more if they broke the law.

But before we could answer, Leilah made the decision easier for us. "Actually, sorry," she said. "They're not home today. But we can go another day?"

That decided the matter. We declined with regret.

*****

For some days afterward, I kept mulling over what Leilah said about the sensuality in Persian culture that necessarily conflicted with the austere and stark desert-born doctrines of Mohammed.

"The word 'paradise,'" she said, "was originally Persian." I looked it up: The old Persian word "*pairidaeza*" as recorded in the Avesta, the collection of Zoroastrian texts, meant "enclosure" or "park." And there was something distinctly indulgent in the Persian park or garden.

The gardens of Shiraz were where I saw the Persian soul show itself more clearly than anywhere else.

Wandering around the Bagh-e Eram ("Garden of Paradise") in this city, I caught sight of a man, sixty or so, reclining on the grass posing for a photo for his wife. The way he supported the weight of his head on his left hand, the left elbow buried in the oily green grass, his fat belly unapologetically straining against the buttons of his shirt, his legs stretched out languidly toward what must've been the edge of the camera frame, and the smile of indulgence on his face, was an image of this sensuality.

In this very ordinary man, I thought I could descry a glimpse of Hafez, perhaps Iran's national poet and Shiraz's favorite son, scribbling his exhilarating if esoteric verses after three or four glasses of that wine named after his hometown.

Elsewhere in the blooming garden young couples made mockery of the mullahs' rules, hiding in the many corners and recesses between hedgerows to hold hands, to talk of love, and perhaps to do much else besides.

*****

Shiraz had my sympathy as the city of sensuality as well as poetry. A part of me wished to linger for no other reason than that. But the Persian Gulf, only a stone's throw away now, beckoned to me as Gan Ying's final stop.

I fell asleep on the bus to the coast. When I woke up, I saw mountains shaped like tents passing by. A river ran beneath them, peculiarly green next to the yellow dustiness. Now and then an old broken bridge spanned it, looking like a relic of the Saracens.

By the time I arrived in oven-hot Bushehr, or Bandar Bushehr (*bandar* meaning "port" in Persian), the sun was leaning westward. I took a walk along the shore, skipping from one rock to the next.

A woman sat alone on a rock before me studying a book. Now and then the salty ocean air delivered a cool burst that just as soon vanished, tantalizing the sweat-covered pedestrian. A pair of fishermen's dinghies bobbed up and down halfway out to sea. Families swam in it. A man spotted me, the foreigner, and waved his arms to invite me to jump into the water with his family. I falsely promised I'd do it the following day. He gestured urgently toward the sea as though saying never put off until tomorrow what fun you can have today. A wave crashed against the rocks and splashed me. The water was as warm as weak tea. In the north end of the peninsular city, a headland jutted out westward with a thousand cargo containers stacked on top of it, colorful, like Lego blocks.

So this was Bushehr.

The *Hou Han Shu* records that Gan Ying reached a Seleucid city named "Tiaozhi," an old Chinese transliteration for "Antiochia" or "Antioch." Numerous cities in the ancient world were thus unimaginatively named after the Seleucid king Antiochus, just as numerous cities were called Alexandria this or Alexandria that after Alexander.

There was an Antioch in Turkey, the one meant in the Bible and today's Antakya. But this was too far from anywhere in the Arsacid empire to have been Gan Ying's final stop, and anyway it lay within Roman territory already. There was an Antioch in Scythia. Its location remained unclear, but Scythia was somewhere in today's Kazakhstan or Turkmenistan or southern Russia, way too far to the north.

Bushehr, however, was called "Antiochia in Persis" — Antioch in Persia — during the reign of the Arsacids, when it remained under Seleucid control. And the *Hou Han Shu* reports Gan Ying's description of the city as being surrounded by water on three sides — a peninsula like Bushehr. Scholars could and still did debate the precise location of "Tiaozhi." But as far as I was concerned, I had my answer: Tiaozhi was Antiochia in Persis, today's Bushehr.

And like the other lost ancient cities that I had chased after, Suyab and Marakanda and Hecatompylos, there was nothing of the old Antioch left. Elamite ruins predating even Persian civilization lay somewhere to the south. But the city of the Seleucids, those descendants of the lieutenants of Alexander, was long gone.

What was here now, what I found, was a modern port that played an uncomfortable host to a nuclear power station a few miles away (a sign hanging over the main road into town announced the direction in which the plant stood). The occasional Russian engineer could be seen around town, helping the Iranians with the project. A local belief, I had read while researching this town, held that the government neglected the infrastructure of Bushehr in the expectation that sooner or later American or Israeli bombs would fall on it from the sky. Lawsuit number three.

Along the shore, though, against the setting sun, there was none of that fear of death from above. There was only fear of death from heatstroke: scientists projected that with climate change, inhuman temperatures would make the shores of the Persian Gulf uninhabitable within a few decades. With my forehead drenched in sweat, I tended to concur. Now and then the sweat got past my eyelids and stung my eyes and made me blink.

Well, it was the way so many lawsuits ended: when everything worth fighting over had been destroyed anyhow, when all the assets at stake had been exhausted, the litigation simply disappeared like a puff of shisha smoke.

Behind me, cars and motorbikes whizzed along the coastal road, noisy and impatient. Yet somehow when I sat down facing the ever-changing water, there was nonetheless a rare measure of peace. The sun reached that angle just above the horizon when it turned impressionistically pink, and shards of that lovely warm color scattered across the surface of the water like so much broken beauty.

I imagined Gan Ying sitting somewhere not too far from where I sat, looking out upon the same sea that I looked upon now, and mulling over his mission. But I was familiar with the ocean, and he was not.

I was born on one island and grew up on another. I come from a postmodern world where humanity has sent space probes past Neptune and Pluto, where to find any location on the surface of this planet all I have to do is to tap on an icon on my phone.

Gan Ying came from the interior of an agrarian country. He lived in an age when the most authoritative work on world geography, the *Shan Hai Jing*, still spoke of fantastical beasts like an animal "with the face of a man, the body of a jackal, the wings of a bird, and the movements of a snake." And it explained solar eclipses as a celestial dog devouring the sun. For that matter, European maps would continue to depict monsters in unknown waters for another fifteen centuries.

Antiochia would have been the first place in his life where Gan Ying saw water like this, water without an apparent end, containing within it all the mysteries of the deep. I found the sight of green waves peaceful. He might have found it terrifying, or at least deeply strange and mysterious.

According to the *Hou Han Shu*, Gan Ying asked the local Persians for directions to Rome. From here the easiest way would have been to cut across Mesopotamia, today's Iraq, to reach the Levant, which during the age of the Antonines was a Roman province. The emperor of Rome at the time was Trajan, the stern soldier and energetic conqueror of Dacia. It would have been a short few weeks' journey, nothing compared to the long distance that Gan Ying had already come from the western sections of the Great Wall.

But they told him to set sail instead and repeated to him the story of the Sirens from the *Odyssey*. The Homeric tale wound up recorded in the pages of the *Hou Han Shu*. And Gan Ying, new to the ocean, believed them and turned around.

Kang Youwei, the late 19th-century Chinese political reformer, once wrote an essay on Gan Ying. He accused him of cowardice for failing to set sail, for being frightened of the ocean, for turning back when he should have forged ahead. For Kang, Gan Ying represented what was wrong with late-imperial China: timidity in the face of change.

But he wasn't being fair. Gan Ying had been a decorated officer in the Han Empire's victorious war against the Huns, one of Ban Chao's thirty-six elite commandos. As a soldier of exemplary military record, he deserves some benefit of the doubt against a charge of cowardice. Kang's writing better represented Chinese anxiety in the age of Western colonialism than an honest assessment of history.

And the *Hou Han Shu* further records that, although Gan Ying failed to reach Rome, he traveled farther than any of his compatriots had ever done, and he brought back knowledge about the outside world that was not even recorded in the scriptures of old, not even in the *Shan Hai Jing*.

Indeed, he brought back an accurate if secondhand description of the Roman Empire itself: "Daqin [Rome]... by the western ocean, spans several thousand *li* [about half a kilometer] and has over four hundred cities. Dozens of small nations serve as vassals. Its city walls are built of stone.... Its people are tall and attractive, like in China, hence the name Daqin [Great China]." He had stepped across so many lines, boundaries that nearly all of his countrymen would have seen as impassable, before he turned back in the face of the final frontier.

So he failed, and yet he succeeded in a way as well.

I sat on the shore in Bushehr staring out onto the sea. Somewhere on the other side of the Gulf lay Kuwait, Saudi Arabia, and the United Arab Emirates. But they were too far to appear on the horizon.

Gan Ying had tried to reach the heart of the Western world, the Eternal City of Rome. I had reached the heart of the Western world of my day, the skyscrapers of New York City. He got turned around in the final stretch, as had I.

And I set out to cross one frontier after another, physically or metaphorically, with my feet or with my mind, traversing and therefore (such was the hope) erasing the boundaries that would divide America from China from Afghanistan from Iran, Christianity from Buddhism from Islam, and the West from the East from the Middle East.

It was a far, far better thing than I had ever done.

I stood back up on the shore of Bushehr. My clothes clung to my body in a suffocating embrace. And yet in that moment I felt a kind of liberation.

7

THE HOUND OF EUROPE

IN BUSHEHR, I had reached Gan Ying's final stop before he turned around and headed back to China. But I couldn't turn back. Neither could I stay here in Iran. I had been running away from that which pursued me down the arches of all these months, and I wasn't about to stop now. The mad dash I made for the finish line now felt truly like an escape attempt — futile though it had to be. No one who tries to flee via the labyrinthine ways of his own soul ever actually succeeds in getting away.

The route that Gan Ying should have taken after Antiochia in Persis, through Mesopotamia to the Levant — today's Iraq and Syria — was not feasible. Instead, if I wished to get to Italy from here without flying, I would have to cross the length of Turkey. And so I did. The panorama of the world outside went by so quickly for a time that it suffices for me to summarize where I passed through.

From the Persian Gulf, I went to Tabriz in northwestern Iran near Armenia and Azerbaijan. From here I crossed the border westward into Turkey. Mt. Ararat, where Noah's Ark supposedly ran aground when the waters of the Flood began to recede, loomed over the border towns on both sides. From here I traversed all of Anatolia, stopping in Erzurum and Cappadocia with its famously strange rock formations and the ancient churches carved into them. Finally reaching the Mediterranean, from the seaside town of Antalya I set sail for Greece.

In Greece my mad dash hit a pause.

After several Aegean islands and Athens, I made my way to the small town of Litochoro near the east coast of mainland Greece. This was base camp for hiking Mt. Olympus, the reason that I'd come. Waking up to the crisp air and cloudless sky one morning, I peered through my window upon the abode of the ancient Greek gods and then set out to climb it.

The path began from quiet Litochoro and wound upward through the tree line gently enough. Through the green foliage of the foothills, I quickly lost sight of the peak, "The Throne of Zeus." For a time, I thought only about the simple act of walking, of putting one foot before the other. For a time, I heard only silence but for my own breathing.

Then: Woof, woof.

I turned and saw a dog wagging his tail several paces behind me. He was a mutt of some sort; I thought I saw half a Labrador in him. In addition to wearing no collar and the unkempt state of his fur, he had appeared alone on this deserted mountain trail, which suggested to me that he had no human. From the solicitous look on his face, I thought maybe he was looking for one.

"Oh hey," I said wearily. "Where the hell did you come from?"

He approached me one step and one wag of the tail at a time, his sloppy tongue sticking out in the cool mountain air. When he got close enough, I put one hand on his head and patted him. He nodded with pleasure and then tried to lick my hand.

"Hey, hey," I withdrew my hand. "I don't know where your tongue has been, buddy."

We spent a few minutes in each other's company like this. "All right," I patted him one last time as I got up to go. "Good boy."

But as I began to continue uphill, he followed me.

"You want to come with me?" I asked. "Well, it's a free country." He sauntered after me joyously as though meeting me was the most exciting thing that had happened to him all day.

"I'm going to call you…" I thought for a minute. I can't say definitively where the idea came from, but come it did, and I settled on a name: "Ignatios."

Man and dog continued the walk. Having four legs instead of two, Ignatios was much faster than I. He ran ahead of me only to double back, over and over, urging me on eagerly, impatiently.

We came upon a clearing in the shadow of a massive rockface. Underneath the overhang stood a small chapel painted sky blue and snow white like the houses on Santorini. For an atheist, I am strangely interested in churches, temples, mosques, and really all things religious. So I walked over to the shrine and discovered that the tiny sanctuary was dedicated to St. Dionysios, a 16th century saint who once resided here as a hermit. In the long centuries after the advent of Christianity, Orthodox Greeks found spirituality here on Mt. Olympus just as their pagan forebears did.

The chapel was built atop a spring, which flowed murmuring and crystalline out of the ground with an inherent sense of the holy. I gathered a palmful of water and splashed it on my face, washing away the accumulating sweat. Behind me, Ignatios sat on his hindquarters and waited for me.

The spring fed into the Epineas River nearby. When we turned away from the chapel and continued on, we soon came upon a river crossing. At the sight of it, Ignatios jumped with joy and then leaped straight into the river, taking care to wag his tag and wiggle his body to maximize the amount of water that he kicked up. On the other side, he ran over to me, made sure I was squarely within the splash zone, and then shook himself dry.

"Come on, man," I said as I wiped the waterdrops from my face. Ignatios responded with more sloppy slathering with his tongue and the biggest if somewhat guilty grin. Post-swim, he was shaggier than ever, but beaming.

How content dogs always are. You never hear a poodle complain that she should've been born a German Shepherd, nor the canine adoptee of one family bemoan not having been adopted by another. If only we humans could learn that same contentment instead of playing over in our minds all that could have been, should have been, might have been.

In this moment, Ignatios looked like being with me was all that he ever wanted in life. And in that purity of heart, he seemed to me nothing less than beatific.

In contrast, look at me with all this running around. One town after another, one country after another. Not too long ago, I was running through some of the most out-of-the-way corners of the world. Now I had returned to what we tend to think of as a "normal" country where normal people went for normal reasons. But still I ran, down the nights and down the days. What was it all for?

I rested one hand on my companion's dome and scratched him behind the ears.

In his Christian mystical poem, "The Hound of Heaven," the British poet Francis Thompson imagined his dissolute person running from a hound. When the hound finally caught up with Thompson, he turned out to be God. And he said:

> *Ah, fondest, blindest, weakest*
> *I am He Whom thou seekest!*
> *Thou dravest love from thee, who dravest me.*

I'm not sure I understand any of that. But here Ignatios had come out of nowhere to befriend me, bringing with him that unalloyed and unconditional affection of which only dogs — and allegedly God — were capable.

No, Ignatios wasn't the Hound of Heaven. And I did not live in a mystical poem of whatever religious persuasion. After hiking up Olympus with me for another hour, Ignatios turned and disappeared amidst the trees just the same way he had come.

But even I, for all my atheism, could sense the divine in this time and place, in the presence of my canine companion, and in the transformative nature of my journey.

*****

Finally, after a ferry ride across the Ionian Sea and a turn through southern Italy, I rode the train northward to my final destination, Rome.

I had been to Rome once before, when I was seventeen. It blew me away on that initial encounter, the first time I traveled internationally without family. The Sistine Chapter, the Pantheon, the Colosseum, the Roman Forum, and all the rest. The sheer grandeur of the city, the stories that every brick and every cobblestone seemed to tell. If I were to look for the beginning of the road that led me to become the person who would take up this quest, then that first, astonishing introduction to the Eternal City would make a good candidate. The road that led me to my education in America, led me to my personal dark forest halfway through life, and finally led me to come here once more.

I ran out to Trajan's Column as soon as I arrived. Trajan was the Roman emperor at the time of Gan Ying's journey. So in my mind I had made this monument the symbolic end point of these months of striving.

But it was already late afternoon. The sun was dipping

westward over the gleaming white memorial of Vittorio Emanuelle nearby. From there it cast a golden light on my final goalpost, endowing it with a romantic hue. The relief depicting the Dacian conquest spiraling upward like a magnificent scroll was just as I remembered. And the copper-green angel still stood on top, overlooking the city in his supercilious attitude.

When I was little and first heard the tale of Gan Ying's mission to Rome, it was always told with a sigh. Who knows how world history might have been different had these two great empires, on two ends of the Eurasian continent, met at this time when both were at the height of their powers? What unimaginable cultural exchange, what spark of ideas, what trade, what confluence of arts and sciences, might have occurred? The most interesting things in this world always happened on boundaries, where different peoples, cultures, and ideas met.

It was not to be. Not then. History is contingent. Life and chance happen to us all.

Several decades after Gan Ying's mission, in 166 A.D., a Roman delegation reached Vietnam, at the time under Chinese suzerainty. But by then, the Han regime was in decline and no longer that strength which in old days moved earth and heaven. Rome itself was only a decade and half away from the accession of the disastrous emperor Commodus and the beginning of the long twilight. Like star-crossed lovers, the two great empires had missed their moment.

I sat down near Trajan's Column and gazed at it bathed in the golden sun, wishing to enjoy this moment of triumph. But is it too obvious to tell you that the moment was short-lived? The exhilaration of success, of having done something grand, faded in a matter of minutes. Unlike the thirty birds who went in search of the holy Simorgh, I didn't suddenly discover that I was the one I'd been looking for all along.

But as I contemplated both the vicissitudes of history that made the world what it is as well as my own peregrinations that had brought me to sitting at this moment on this slab of marble in Rome, a Daoist fable from the Han Dynasty came to mind. Here's my translation of the original 2nd century B.C. text:

> There is a man who lives near the Great Wall who has knowledge of fortune-telling. One day his horses run away into the land of the Huns. People come to give their condolences. But the man says, "Who is to say it's not good fortune?" A few months later, his horses return with a great many tall and strong Hunnish horses. People come to congratulate him. But the man says, "Who is to say it's not bad fortune?" As his household is now wealthy with good horses, his son comes to love riding. One day the son falls from a horse and breaks his thigh. People come to give their condolences. The father says, "Who is to say it's not good fortune?" A year later, the Huns launch a massive invasion across the border. All able-bodied young men who live near the fortress have to pick up a bow and join the army. Out of every ten men, nine die. But his son is exempt because he is a cripple. Father and son both survive the war. Thus you see that in good luck lies disaster, and disaster transmutes into good luck. The mysteries of fate are beyond human comprehension.

There is no telling how history might have turned out differently had Gan Ying reached Rome, whether it would've been for the better or for the worse. The same is true in our own age: Who was to say how the American adventure in

Afghanistan would ultimately end? Who was to say what its ultimate consequences would be fifty, a hundred, or a thousand years into the future?

And the same is true in our individual lives. No one could've foreseen that my choice so many years ago to study in America would put me on a path leading here, to the end of a long journey across Eurasia. And no one could foresee now whither the path might continue, what I would yet do, where I might yet be, for better or for worse. For the mysteries of fate are truly beyond human comprehension.

And if it is for the worse?

Peter Matthiessen recounts his climbs up and down the Himalayas in a laborious attempt to catch a glimpse of the eponymous animal in his book, *The Snow Leopard*. Toward the end of his expedition, having failed to spot the elusive big cat, Matthiessen visited a remote Tibetan monastery. There lived a Lama who, immobilized by bad legs, could never leave the lamasery. As tactfully as he could, Matthiessen asked the Lama if he was happy with his isolation.

"Of course I am happy here!" replied the holy man. "It's wonderful! *Especially* when I have no choice!"

It was a moment of epiphany for Matthiessen, this lesson in the acceptance of what is.

"Have you seen the snow leopard?"

"No! Isn't that wonderful?"

I got back up, took one last longing look at Trajan's Column, and walked away. Onto the next thing, the next day, the next city, the next journey.

Maybe my future endeavors will all miscarry. Maybe the next day will turn out disastrously. Maybe the next city will be no fun at all. And maybe I'll find nothing rewarding on the next journey.

Or maybe just the opposite.

Either way, the trick is to say: "Isn't that wonderful!"

If I could learn to embrace life with all its ups and downs as it is rather than what I wished it were, then it might yet be the beginning of wisdom.

FROM THE WALL TO THE WATER

ABOUT THE AUTHOR

William Han was born in Taiwan and grew up in New Zealand before receiving his education at Yale University and Columbia Law School. As well as a travel writer and lawyer, he is a screenwriter and occasional journalist. He has been to over 120 countries and divides his time between here, there, and everywhere.